UNIVERSITY CHARTER SCHOOL STUDENTS

Wisdom Writers:

Volume 3

Copyright © 2024 by University Charter School Students

All rights reserved. No part of this publication may be reproduced, stored or transmitted in any form or by any means, electronic, mechanical, photocopying, recording, scanning, or otherwise without written permission from the publisher. It is illegal to copy this book, post it to a website, or distribute it by any other means without permission.

University Charter School Students asserts the moral right to be identified as the author of this work.

University Charter School Students has no responsibility for the persistence or accuracy of URLs for external or third-party Internet Websites referred to in this publication and does not guarantee that any content on such Websites is, or will remain, accurate or appropriate.

First edition

Editing by Ana S. Montaño Alanis
Cover art by Emonie Rush
Advisor: Tamaya Tolliver
Advisor: Charle Ryland
Advisor: Avery Long

This book was professionally typeset on Reedsy.
Find out more at reedsy.com

Contents

Foreword   x
Preface   xiii

I   Our School

ACCOMPLISHMENTS IN SCHOOL	3
Hannah Price	4
Traeger Stephens	5
IRRITATION FROM PEERS	6
Aliyah Martin	7
Zy'Kirea Long	8
Hannah Price	9
Angel Burrell	10
Addyson Tillman	11
Anonymous	12
Anonymous	14
Clint McDonald	16
HIGH SCHOOL & MIDDLE SCHOOL EXPERIENCES	17
Zy'Kirea Long	18
Anonymous	19
Jaylon Amerson	21
Tratavein Collins	22
I WANT TO LEARN	23
Kayla Harris	24
Avery Long	26

Avery Long	28
Aliyah Martin	31
Angel Burrell	32
CHARACTER EDUCATION TRAITS	33
Anonymous	34
James Edmonds	36
Colton Burg	37
Kayla Harris	39
LAWS OF LIFE	42
Amarion Dubose	43
Ella Hill	44
Preston Irby	46
Ana S. Montaño Alanis	47
Colton Burg	49
Zamiyah Rice	51
Anonymous	53
Craig Ellington	55
Anonymous	56
Kareem Elnaham	58
Madison Love	59
Zy'Keria Long	60
Hannah Price	62
Addyson Tillman	63
Tamaya Tolliver	64
Jamiya Jenkins	66
Mathew Kendrick	68
DEAR 7TH GRADE SELF	70
Amarion Dubose	71
Zy'Kirea Long	72
Zamiyah Rice	73
Matthew Buck	75

James Edmonds	76
Craig Ellington	77
Anonymous	79
Gradon Fike	80
Anonymous	82
Ryan Vaughan	84
Madison Love	85
Anonymous	86
Anonymous	88
SPORTS	90
Yazmine McAboy	91
NARRATIVE 4 EXPERIENCE	93
Avery Long	94
Kayla Harris	96
Angel Burrell	97
POSITIVE AND NEGATIVE ASPECTS OF HIGH SCHOOL	98
Amarion Dubose	99
James Edmonds	101
Kareem Elnaham	102
Jamiya Jenkins	103
Mathew Kendrick	104
Yazmine McAboy	105
Zamiyah Rice	106
Addyson Tillman	107
Tamya Tolliver	108

II Our Lives

HOLIDAYS & TRADITIONS	113
Emily Walker	114
Clint McDonald	116

Kayla Harris	117
Anonymous	119
Tavares Foster	121
MY PLACE	122
Emily Walker	123
Avery Long	125
Aliyah Martin	127
Hannah Prince	129
Traeger Stephens	131
Anonymous	132
LEARNING EXPERIENCE	134
Lennon Phillips	135
Amarion Dubose	136
Matthew Kendrick	138
Zy'Kirea Long	140
Hannah Price	142
Zamiyah Rice	144
Addyson Tillman	145
Angel Burrell	147
Emily Walker	148
WHEN DID YOU LAST…	150
Shaquon Lee	151
Ana S. Montaño Alanis	152
Ana S. Montaño Alanis	154
TEENS	156
Sadie Carter	157
Justin Clarke	158
A.J.	159
MUSIC & ART	161
Angel Burrell	162
Tavares Foster	164

Kayla Harris	165
Emily Walker	167
Anonymous	169
Jaylon Amerson	171
Zy'Kirea Long	172
Jamya James	173
Addyson Tillman	174
TRAVEL	176
Matthew Kendrick	177
Amarion Dubose	179
Zy'Kirea Long	181
Tamaya Tolliver	182
EFFECTS OF SOCIAL MEDIA	184
Yazmine McAboy	185
Zamiyah Rice	186
Tamya Tolliver	187
Amarion Dubose	188
Kamyia Dubose	189
James Edmonds	190
Matthew Kendrick	191
Addyson Tillman	192
POSITIVE EFFECTS OF PANDEMIC RESTRICTIONS	193
Kayla Harris	194

III Ourselves

POEMS	199
Anonymous	200
Addisyn Barton	202
Ana S. Montaño Alanis	203
Ana S. Montaño Alanis	207

Rebecca Boydstun	209
Rebecca Boydstun	210
Rebecca Boydstun	211
Rebecca Boydstun	213
Rebecca Boydstun	215
FEARS & ANXIETIES	218
Angel Burell	219
Anonymous	221
Kayla Harris	223
Zy'Kirea Long	226
Aliyah Martin	227
Ana S. Montaño Alanis	228
Hannah Prince	230
Traeger Stephens	232
Avery Long	233
Tavares Foster	234
Leia Pitre	235
Addyson Tillman	236
A.J.	238
Zamiyah Rice	240
Caroline Sparkman	241
Zy'Kirea Long	242
Amarion Dubose	243
Ana S. Montaño Alanis	245
INSECURITIES & BODY IMAGE	248
Hannah Prince	249
Kayla Harris	250
Hannah Prince	252
Angel Burrell	253
PASSIONS	254
Avery Long	255

Ana S. Montaño Alanis	256
FAMILY & HOME LIFE	260
Anonymous	261
Anonymous	264
Avery Long	266
Ana S. Montaño Alanis	268
LOSS	271
Aliyah Martin	272
Caroline Sparkman	273
Acknowledgments	274

Foreword

We've seen it all and we're still moving.

Like all histories, it's best to begin at the very beginning, and for West Alabama this means we start with the Choctaw Nation.

Sumter County, and western Alabama in general, is a mainly rural region covered in pastureland, fields of flowers, rolling hills, and cliffs of pure white limestone, a land that has brought explorers and travelers here since DeSoto explored this land over 400 years ago. A land which feels as if time as stopped, yet is quietly progressing forwards, a land rich in resources, yet not in capital, a land which lays upon the River of the Coffin Makers, 20 and 17, these numbers mean so much to those traveling long distances, or just stopping into town for groceries. This is what we know as home, number 60, and we represent it with pride. Throughout the earliest years post Treaty of Dancing Rabbit, the land was mainly, no, entirely agriculturally dependent, yet it was a flourishing land, river boats sailed the waters of the Bigbee, from steam sternwheelers to a gumtree canoe under the light of the moon, bringing commerce to the towns of Gainesville, Epes, and McDowell.

In 1861, the state seceded from the nation, a republic born and fell within months, soon, a great power rose, and the Southern Wind roared to life, though to tame it took many men, much hardship, it was still done, marching to take on the Queen City of Mississippi, boys in blue rolled over the communities of Pickens and Sumter Counties, then all was quiet. Reconstruction could now begin a new life for those of the South, a hopeful one at that. From the 1850s to today roads not of tar or dirt, but iron and nickel, have rolled along our hills and forests, connecting the Queen and Crescent with the Phoenix and Pittsburgh of the South, the hammer of the drivers, the roar of a whistle, the rattle of a boxcar car, and the hum of a General Electric or Electro Motive Division motor, the towns that grew up along these trade roots are still prevalent today, might not be in the grand scheme of the world, yet we know them, and you can probably name them too. The Alabama Great Southern, the Southern, our own Alabama, Tennessee, and Northern, the Sumter and Choctaw and its little steamers, to the giants of the Midwest, the Frisco and BN, they all have rolled through at one time or another, and now all that is left is the Thoroughbred, a merger of the railroad that Served the South, and the line which hauled the coal to the coast. Back in the day my great grandfather ran the line of the Selma line, York to Selma, a line which is almost completely forgotten to all, like the rest, but not to me. When the wars came, our men were sent, when hard times reared their head, we stuck together through thick and thin. We sure have stayed to our roots, but we're growing, from agriculture to business, we're at the center of it all, bringing in industry to the destitute, bringing in fame for a region.

From War Eagle to Roll Tide, Go Big Blue and Go Tigers, culture still abounds, the weekends bringing in the games that gather crowds, that people like my mother sit down and watch for hours, rooting for the home team, might not always win, but has that ever stopped us? Did it stop us when war came, when the railroads left? Did we ever believe that through it all we were never going to succeed? I'll ask you this: When has a proud Alabamian ever said quit when the going gets tough, when the road becomes rocky, and when the rains fall, no, when the rough gets rougher, the Alabamians get tougher. That's why I'm here, that's why I'm able to say that we've been here, been here for nearly 7 generations, and we aren't planning on giving up on Alabama anytime soon. Our region has been blessed by the Lord above with resources which have given rise to our towns, our landmarks, and that's why every Sunday morning, we head to the old white church on the hill, sing praises, and talk of what's gone on that week. That's where we gather, may it be a church, the Bakery, Jim's, Austin's, no matter where it may be, when we get together, you better prepare for some gossip and hearing just about everything under the Sun. Yet, that's what I love, listening to what's gone on, to the elderly and their stories and jokes, it makes me smile, and for every mile of this land, I find quite a bit that makes me smile. There's always something along the way to make your day, no matter how dark it may be, or how high the heat rises, this is Sumter County, and am I sure glad to be right where I am today.

Author: Wyatt Dial

Preface

If you've ever felt like you're trapped in a box, then perhaps you are familiar with what I'm going to talk about.

I was going to write about something completely different. Maybe how I've been affected by bullying, or by my family, or about moments in my life, like the topics suggested. But I've come to realize that the story I want to tell is hidden in every story I've told, and the message I want to impart is so much greater than that. It's a lesson I've only learned recently. I want to ask you this:

Why should we define our lives and dreams by the expectations set for us by other people?

I read a book about this recently. It's called Gap Life by John Coy. I'll give you a quick run-down; a recent high school graduate named Cray doesn't want the life of a doctor his father has set out for him, and decides instead to take a gap year. It's a coming-of-age story at its purest: a teen growing into an adult and learning valuable lessons along the way. I'm sure some people in here have read a similar story.

I think it's interesting that I read this book when I did. I don't believe in fate or destiny, but I think I knew what I was doing when I plucked this book from my bookshelves and placed it in my backpack. I'm glad I did. I learned a lot from it, and Gap Life comes highly recommended to anyone looking for a good book.

But the lesson Cray practices over the course of the book is the lesson I want to teach: The only type of success that will make anyone happy is the success they set for themselves. What each person defines as successful, not the society around them. Let me ask you a question: did you write the rules for your life? Did you set the expectations, purposefully, personally? The answer is probably no, because the truth is, most people don't. The truth of our society is that we are not generally trusted to set our own definitions of success, especially when there are other people who seem have more knowledge on the matter preaching the meaning of success.

This "meaning of success" is usually wealth and power in the business world, or making some huge discovery that will be remembered for centuries. But how does anyone ever truly know what success is for someone else, especially someone they don't even know exists? What if that's not the path you want? What if you want something more personal, something that lights a fire in your heart, something you love doing?

It always seems that this dream is devalued by society. After all, isn't it just small-minded and small-scaled, a lack of drive, of ambition?

Isn't it a lesser dream?

No, it's not.

How can a dream be lesser than another when each dreamer wants theirs the same?

Author: Charle Ryland

I

Our School

ACCOMPLISHMENTS IN SCHOOL

Hannah Price

The first thing I accomplished this school year was passing the CPR test for Nurse Jenny. It wasn't a big test but it was very important. You couldn't miss more than 3 questions. If you did, you failed the test. There were 25 questions on the test. I was very nervous about taking it. Also, the CPR check was easy. It was a lot of work to save an adult, child, and infant, and you had to make sure you did it right. I never thought I would pass the CPR check-off and test so I am very proud of myself for that. I prayed to the Lord about the test to lead and guide me through it.

Traeger Stephens

I have met my goal of having an 80% or higher in my classes. I have also accomplished getting my driver's license. I took driver's education with Coach Walker Lewis last year. It taught me how to turn my tires toward the curb while parking on a hill. My mom helped me get my license online. It felt really good, and I was really happy to be able to drive wherever I wanted to go. I like being able to get fast food whenever I want, Little Ceaser's being my favorite place to drive to get food from. I like being able to drive people around in my truck, too. I feel like I was ready and responsible enough to drive at 17 years old.

I also became CPR certified with Nurse Jenny this semester. I liked this process better this year because I only had to use my hands instead of breathing in the mannequin's mouth. I feel like I may be able to save someone's life now. Even though this was for a grade, I feel like I learned a lot, and this experience will help me in life.

IRRITATION FROM PEERS

Aliyah Martin

Yes, some of the students in my class intentionally irritate me. I get triggered when people talk over me or someone else because I don't enjoy it when people talk over me. I also find it annoying when people tap things on my desk or make distracting noises. For you and those around you who are trying to work, that is a distraction. It also irritates me when students disobey their teachers' directions and interrupt class since it is impolite to both the teachers and the students who are attempting to learn. You know that your parents did not send you to school so you could play and make jokes. I usually find these males in my fourth block class to be very obnoxious. The teacher continuously warns them to stop talking and laughing, but they never stop and never finish any work. They won't learn by horseplaying, so the instructor must always raise her voice to get them to behave and pay attention. She always needs to stop what she's doing and fuss at them, which really irritates me while everyone else is attempting to learn.

Zy'Kirea Long

I get really upset when a teacher tells a student to get in their seat, and the student gets an attitude with the teacher. Students can be so disrespectful for no reason. Other students get on my nerves when I'm trying to do my work and they just keep tapping on me while I work. I get upset when I'm helping someone with schoolwork, and they just sit there.

I get upset when a student lies about me doing something I had no idea about. It is a very low thing to do. I get upset when some students think everything is funny when it's not. Their constant laughter and remarks make my head hurt. Smacking in my ear gets on my nerves because these kids will lean over to you and just smack. Something else that gets on my nerves is when students are being mean to these teachers for no reason. It makes me feel so mad. There is this girl in my class, and she just grabs my sleeves and hits me. It gets on my nerves and it's so annoying.

Hannah Price

Yes! Some students will make unnecessary comments and noises. They will horseplay around when you are trying to focus on your work. It's very hard to tell them to stop playing around because they won't listen at all. That's why I just let a teacher handle it because they will stop at that moment. They do things that are funny when we are doing work, but sometimes they can take it too far. Also, the noises! The blurt-out noises out of nowhere are very childish. They will do it when it's quiet in the classroom and it's very annoying. Although, it is mostly the boys. The girls don't do anything at all. We can sometimes be loud, but not all the time. But that always gets on my nerves.

Angel Burrell

In my class, some of the students kind of get on my nerves. They do unnecessary things that shouldn't be done. One thing that most people do a lot is disrespect the teachers when they are trying to get the class quiet or trying to explain something. In my opinion, I think that is very disrespectful because you wouldn't want anyone to disrespect you. Treat people the way you would want to be treated.

Another point I would say is students showing disrespect when a teacher is teaching, and the students laying their heads down. If you see that your teacher is talking about something important, don't just lay your head down like you don't hear them talking. I say that because if you were standing up and saying something important, you would want all the attention focused on you. Students are very disrespectful nowadays because they think it is funny and cool. Being disrespectful gets you nowhere.

The last thing that irritates me is when the teacher leaves the room, the class tries to get loud and act up. You're making yourself look bad instead of the teacher. The teacher already has a good background. Most students do activities like this because they are convinced to do them by their friends.

Addyson Tillman

Students in my class always get on my nerves. I like the class, but some of the kids make it absolutely unbearable, and it gets overwhelmingly noisy and very loud. Don't get me wrong, the subject of the class and the teacher are great, I just sometimes cannot handle it. It gets me overwhelmed very quickly, and I just cannot leave.

For example, we had a sub one day, and our class just kept talking and talking. They would not be quiet, nor would they listen to the substitute teacher. I do not want to specify names, and I won't, but I wish these practical young adults would stop acting like four-year-old children. They are perfectly capable of listening and following certain directions and rules we're given. It is honestly ridiculous, and if I had to pick, a few of these students would be gone. I love this class – don't get me wrong. It just sometimes feels like a chore. It feels like taking care of disobedient kids, without actually being the caretaker. Going back to when I mentioned that I could not just leave the class, I have actually considered doing just that, because the noise is, once again, unbearable. I honestly and admittedly admire our teacher. She is doing the best she can, and I love that for her.

Anonymous

Dear class,
I am delighted to know you all, even if we don't get along. I enjoy speaking to you all on the days y'all do not act outrageous. I have been a part of Wisdom Writers since Volume 1. We had the perfect class and had no distractions. This past year has been nothing but awful in this class. The course and teacher itself are nothing but amazing. The students, not so much. I wish you wouldn't disrespect your peers and teacher. I wish you wouldn't talk and yell when Mrs. Allen asks you not to. I wish you would stay and sit in your ASSIGNED seats and not get up unless instructed. I wish you would do your work and write in class so we can build and write Volume 3. I wish you wouldn't act out at the end of the day and make people cry in their cars when going home. It's so frustrating when you have classmates who do not respect their teachers or classmates, don't do work, and act like they can do anything they want to. Why do you all curse so much when in class? Why act out when Mrs. Allen goes to the bathroom or the office? Why be awful and not listen to substitutes when your teacher is gone? You don't control and own the classroom or school, so don't act like you do. You are very disruptive. There are very few students who try to do our work or make up some type of work we didn't finish, but can't concentrate because you all can't quiet yourselves. We have asked over and over OURSELVES for y'all

ANONYMOUS

to be quiet or to listen and y'all don't. Why do you all have to be so disruptive and disrespectful? It isn't hard to do what you're supposed to do. I pray for each of you all night that you wake up one day and decide that today is the day to change yourselves for the better.

Sincerely,
Your Fellow Dive Class Peer

Anonymous

Dear DIVE class,
   You irk me and frustrate me to no known end. Your behaviors in my opinion are entirely disrespectful, vexing, disrupting, inappropriate, and, most of all, ugly. With there being only six people who do not make my blood boil beneath my skin, myself and the teacher included, I find that this class is the one I dislike much more than others. It is not for a lack of good material or that I simply do not like the subject, but because the children in this class are detestable and borderline wretched.

I find your blatant vulgarity and continuous disrespect for our teacher disgusting. Mrs. Allen is nothing but kind and patient with you, and I feel you take advantage of her kinder nature and flexibility. Ron Clark is credited with saying, "Anyone can be taught." And I agree, but this only applies to those who wish to learn and have a drive to better themselves, an ideal that you children do not seem to embrace.

You curse, back-talk, play on your devices, skimp out on work, run around the class, act like fools, and ignore the bare minimum of work that would allow you to succeed. You do not listen and would rather cut the rope lowered down to help you reach the top than comply with any authority other than the false comfort of your "friends'" opinions. While friends are well and good, the company you keep is reflected by your actions. Therefore, you are either friends with beasts or idolize delinquent behavior exhibited by your peers.

I would love to say that you'll grow out of it, that you will change and calm down in the years to come, but that would mean you hadn't stomped the last sprig of faith I had in you. Even if I am the only person to say this, I shall. You disappoint me. Your actions and your choices disappoint me. I would hope you work towards betterment in the future, as the way you treat yourselves and the people around you disgusts me not only as a classmate but as a person who has an interest in becoming a teacher. I pray that one day you will decide to do better, to be better, but it may be for naught.

I encourage you to learn compassion and integrity, which may help later.

Clint McDonald

People spit on me when I was younger, and they would scream in my ears. This was at Livingston Junior High School, in 2011-2012. They did this just to irritate me. I tried to either ignore them or annoy them back.

There is one student now who really irritates me. He tries to act gangsta, and it is cringy. He begs for my food at lunch, the whole I'm trying to eat. He has food for his lunch but will not leave me alone to eat peacefully. He always tries to get me to play top hand, a slapping game with our hands. Most of my teachers don't allow this game to be played in their classes. So, sometimes I get in trouble for this. I get annoyed when he talks loud. He is so loud all day. I wish he would talk quietly. Sometimes he tries to sit by me, and I let him because I'm trying to be nice. That is the type of person I am: nice.

HIGH SCHOOL & MIDDLE SCHOOL EXPERIENCES

Zy'Kirea Long

My first year of high school was terrible in my eyes. Mentally, I was not ready for high school. I was being mean to all my teachers. I was just not stable enough for high school work. In the second or first week of school, I wasn't getting any work done in English because I was laughing with friends. I was always going off of what other people said about that teacher. The day we got to the English Class, we had a seating chart. That day, I was "mean mugging," just being mean. We had our seats changed, but if we did not want to sit there, we had to write a note. I bumped her head with that note because I did not think how Mrs. Allen would feel. I said very hurtful things to her that day, all because I wanted to sit with my friends. Not even a whole year later, I love her so much. I feel like Mrs. Allen gave me another chance because she was still nice to me even after that. I did not understand why.

Different colors mean a lot to me, but the color green really means something because I have a green person. A green person is someone who saved me—a person who randomly became a big part of my life and just saved me from myself. My green person is Mrs. Allen because I just feel like she's my safe place. I feel like she sees me, and she makes me feel understood. I can tell her anything without being judged. Mrs. Allen holds a special place in my life and heart, and I'd never replace her. I never want her to leave.

Anonymous

On Tuesday and Thursday, two boys, who are both 18 and therefore young men, decided to harass me in Agricultural Science. They were asking and saying inappropriate things to me accompanied by asking me out multiple times after I had already said no. I thought that reporting these boys to Mrs. May and Coach Brandon would make them leave me alone or, at least, stop talking to me about those things, but the main aggressor seemed to now believe I was over-exaggerating and got him in trouble for no reason. I am tired of this boy talking bad about me while sitting directly behind me and I'm tired of him pretending it was a harmless joke.

It wasn't harmless, and he *has* and *is* making me feel bad on purpose for reporting what he and his friend did. I felt very uncomfortable and unsafe. Both boys being inappropriate made me feel terrible inside and about myself. I am not a joke, and I am not over-exaggerating, and I'm tired of them treating me as if I am a joke. I thought they would grow up and maybe act as if they are almost grown men, but it is becoming evermore clear to me that they are either entirely without empathy and respect or that they do not take anything they do seriously.

I want to go home and I want to scream. Yet I'm not going home. I am just fated to cry in the bathroom stall because I'll never want to give them the satisfaction of seeing how much they upset me. Even today, they are still bothering me. The boy who was the main aggressor is now telling anyone who'll listen that I lied and that I should learn to take a joke. The thing about a good joke is that everyone laughs, and when you tell a teacher, your friends, and even your family, they don't look like they're about to throw up and go to war on your behalf.

It baffles me to no end that this behavior comes from two boys who are not only seniors, my classmates, and people whom my friends have known for years, but also boys who love football and want a good career. But maybe I *am* asking too much of them when I ask them to stop and be respectful to me. I hope one day they can learn to be kind and respectful, because you get what you put into the world, and at the rate they're going, they will find a much worse situation than just being harassed.

Jaylon Amerson

When I was in middle school, I took a knife to school because I was trying to be like other people and like other students. I pulled it out, waved it around, and played with it. One student told the teacher I had a knife. When the teacher asked who, he pointed my way. I tried to lie out of it. Before I went to the principal's office, I hid the knife close so I would know where it was. I arrived at his office and he asked me If I had a knife. I said no. He asked, "Why the students say you had a knife?" He asked where it was, and I insisted I didn't have one. I kept lying and asked if he was going to suspend me. He said he wouldn't suspend me if I got the knife and gave it to him. He called my mother, and she came to the school. I got in trouble because she took the knife from me after I retrieved it. I couldn't go to school for the rest of the school year, and I learned from that. Don't be like other people. Be yourself, and don't try to impress others. I stopped hanging out with bad influence people and started doing my work. I would play and joke with friends but still do my work, listen to my teachers, and respect others. But sometimes, I can be rude if I'm having a bad day. Sometimes, I need my time to myself.

Tratavein Collins

In 7th grade, I knew stuff about essays. I knew stuff about different types of languages. I knew stuff about fairy tales, and I knew the work in 7th grade would be complicated. I learned that I would need to study at home and in my free time.

I wish I had done more math homework. Math was really hard at first, but I asked for help and Ms. Webb helped me. In 7th grade (and really any student), one should always ask for help. There will always be someone at school who can help. I wish I had done my work on time instead of waiting until the last day of school. Everyone was having fun at the end of school, except me.

I wish I had followed UCS rules the whole year. I was in several fights. One time, someone hit me in my stomach while playing basketball, and I hit him in the face. I wish I had stopped and told a coach or teacher.

Be responsible! I learned how to organize my notebooks and my backpack. This helped me keep up with papers for each class. In the second semester, after trying to be responsible, I became more successful.

I WANT TO LEARN

Kayla Harris

I've always been raised on the idea that there is a Heaven and Hell (not by choice), that good people go to Heaven, or those who follow God, and bad people go to Hell, those who don't. There was one experience during my philosophy class earlier this year that kind of made me start to think about what "I" believed in. We were having this sort of off-topic discussion about something religion-related and incorporating morality in it, I think. Some students were arguing about how some things did and didn't make sense in the Bible. I can't remember everything that we talked about, but my teacher eventually asked one of the students, *"How can God punish and send someone to hell for simply not knowing of him?"* When he asked this, in my head, I agreed with him because it didn't make sense to me as well. I don't know why, but it just made me more inclined to think and wonder about spiritual things and the afterlife for myself.

So, to answer the prompt, I wish I could learn about the afterlife in school. I've always been fascinated by concepts of life after death, the soul, and the spiritual world, but I've rarely had the opportunity to explore these topics in depth. I think understanding the afterlife could help me appreciate life more and give me a deeper understanding of my place in the universe. I'm interested in learning more because I want to discover more about the meaning of my existence and what happens to me after death. I want to know if there is an afterlife and how it works, what happens to my soul, and whether or not I believe in reincarnation.

I also believe that understanding the afterlife could bring a sense of closure and healing. Those who have suffered the sudden loss of a loved one could gain reassurance that they may find peace or reunion after death. Those who have faced traumas or hardships could find hope that life continues beyond this life and that their loved ones are still with them. Overall, I believe learning more about the afterlife can provide comfort, closure, and healing to people grappling with difficult or traumatic experiences.

Avery Long

School is a thing in life that all kids must go through that allows and helps kids develop and become better citizens. All American high school students must take different classes, which are considered "core classes." This includes Math, History, English, and Science. These classes may be important, but what about after high school when you go out into the real world? When you become an adult and suddenly must know how to write a check, do taxes, buy a home or car?

How are we supposed to know how to do all these things when they don't teach it in school? One thing I wish I could learn in school is doing taxes. I wish there was a class that breaks down all the things that go into it. In English, we have tried going over taxes and understanding them, but I am still confused. In my opinion, I want a class that goes over details and helps you understand more about taxes.

What is the purpose of doing taxes though? Why do I want to learn this particular skill? Taxes provide revenue for federal, local, and state governments to fund essential services—defense, highways, police, a justice system—that benefit all citizens, who could not provide such services very effectively for themselves. I want to learn more about doing taxes because I have no clue in the world how to do them. Understanding how taxation works can give you a big-picture idea about the ways your money gets taxed and empower you to take greater control of your finances. A financial advisor can help you align your tax strategies to reach your financial goals.

Avery Long

The Importance of Career Prep as a High School Student

Career preparation should be a required component of every high school student's education since it provides them with critical skills and information for future success. To begin, career preparation assists students in exploring their interests, abilities, and limitations, helping them to make educated judgments about their future pathways. Many children start high school with little exposure to other occupations, and a career prep program may be a great tool for self-discovery.

Second, including career preparation in the high school curriculum develops students' sense of purpose and drive. Students can better comprehend the value of their education and how it relates to their career objectives by linking classroom learning to real-world applications. This link can instill a better work ethic and dedication to academic success, preparing students for the obstacles they will confront in their chosen careers.

Furthermore, job preparation workshops teach important life skills such as resume writing, interview strategies, and effective communication. These abilities are not only useful in the working world, but they also help with personal growth. Students who receive this type of training are more prepared to negotiate the job market, stand out to potential employers, and develop successful careers. These talents are transferable regardless of the precise job route chosen by a student, making career preparation generally valuable.

A complete career prep class should be designed to integrate both theoretical knowledge and practical practice. Career exploration, goal-setting, and the development of employable skills can all be covered in the classroom. Hands-on activities, internships, and mentoring programs may all give students real-world experience in their chosen industries at the same time. This dual approach guarantees that students not only learn the theoretical parts of their prospective occupations but also acquire practical experience that improves their workforce preparation.

Furthermore, career prep programs should be dynamic and adaptive in order to accommodate students' different interests and ambitions. Individualized career counseling sessions can assist students in developing individualized strategies based on their talents and goals. Guest speakers from a variety of professions can provide insights into various career pathways, providing a more complete picture of the choices available. The education system may better prepare students for the increasingly competitive and dynamic job market they will enter after graduation by personalizing the class to the requirements of each student.

Finally, forcing high school students to attend job preparation programs prior to graduation is critical for their overall growth and future success. The class should be carefully designed to combine theoretical knowledge with practical experiences, fostering self-discovery, motivation, and the acquisition of necessary life skills. By adding career preparation into the high school curriculum, educational institutions may enable students to make educated decisions about their futures and confidently navigate the intricacies of the

WISDOM WRITERS:

professional world.

Aliyah Martin

Something I wish I could learn in school is practical financial literacy. While schools often teach basic arithmetic skills, they may not emphasize the importance of budgeting, investing, and understanding credit. Learning how to manage money wisely is a crucial life skill that I believe would benefit students greatly in their future endeavors. By providing a solid foundation in financial literacy, schools could empower students to make informed decisions and set themselves up for long-term financial success.

Additionally, I wish the school would offer more comprehensive courses on mental health and well-being. While academic subjects are undoubtedly important, the focus on mental health education could help students cope with stress, develop resilience, and foster healthy relationships. Understanding the basics of mental health and emotional intelligence could improve students' individual well-being and contribute to a more supportive and empathetic school community overall.

Finally, schools should incorporate more practical life skills into their curriculum. From basic home maintenance and car care to cooking and nutrition, teaching these skills in school could better prepare students for independent living. By learning these practical life skills, students could develop self-sufficiency and confidence in handling everyday tasks, setting them up for success in adulthood.

Angel Burrell

I think that one of the most important things that we should learn more about in school is critical thinking. This skill involves being able to analyze information, draw conclusions, and form arguments in a logical, reasonable way. It is essential for navigating life decisions, evaluating arguments, and making informed decisions. In addition, understanding critical thinking skills can help us communicate effectively, solve problems, and make better use of our resources. By learning more about critical thinking in school, we can better prepare ourselves for the future and make more informed decisions that will benefit ourselves, our communities, and the world.

Critical thinking encourages the development of many crucial skills, such as logical thinking, decision-making, and open-mindedness. When we think critically, we think on our own as we trust ourselves more. That's why critical thinking, in my opinion, should be brought into schools more. This topic could help students improve their critical thinking skills and learn more knowledge about the topic.

Critical thinking is at the forefront of learning, as it aids a student to reflect and understand their point of view. This skill helps a student figure out how to make sense of the world, based on personal observation and understanding. Critical thinking is crucial, not just for learning, but for life overall! Education isn't just a way to prepare ourselves for life. It's life itself.

CHARACTER EDUCATION TRAITS

Anonymous

Responsibility:
As a Charter School, we do something called houses with each having a character trait implemented with each house. Aside from the houses, we have character traits each month and at the end of that month, we give out rewards for the students who exemplify that trait at school.

A character trait that I find easiest and think is my best is responsibility. I show responsibility by getting to school on time and showing up in classes on time. I do all my schoolwork even if it is hard. I push myself to do that schoolwork so I don't fall behind. I also turn in my schoolwork on time. In class, we have due dates. If the work is not on time, it gets counted as half a grade, not a full one. Another example of me being responsible is that if I am out during the week for a day or two, I always go to my peers and teachers and ask what work I missed and how I can get caught up. Being responsible seems hard to my peers sometimes, and I don't understand how.

Although I struggle with patience, I get confused about how they struggle with responsibility. Patience is one of the hardest things for me to have. Especially when I have two classes where more than half the class gets on my nerves. I have practiced patience by taking deep breaths or even walking to the bathroom for a break. Without doing that and having patience, I have lashed out in the past and yelled at my classmates for not listening to the teachers or respecting the adults in the classroom.

Having no patience will get me nowhere in life. As a senior in High School and wanting to be a special ed teacher in the future, I need to learn and grow more patience. I have struggled with this in the past especially at home with family. If someone doesn't do something when I ask them right then and there, I will get upset and angry. I am so thankful for learning more patience, but as I struggle, I hope to grow more.

James Edmonds

Patience:

Patience is very important in life. Here are two things about patience. With patience, life will be more relaxed. Whenever you have something, and you rush it, it makes it more stressful, so you need to be more patient. Another time I need patience is when I do my favorite thing, hunting. I need patience in both types of hunting I do, which is deer hunting and duck hunting. I need patience when I am deer hunting because every time I go hunting, I am waiting for a big deer to walk out. I also need patience when deer hunting cause when the big deer walks out, I need to stay on it to get in range or turn for me to get a shot on it. Another time in hunting I need patience is when I am duck hunting. There are two ways I show patience when duck hunting. The first is when I am hunting, and I am at the duck hole, and there are no ducks at the moment. I need to be more patient and wait when there are not many ducks. The second reason I need patience in duck hunting is when the ducks are circling, and people are calling, and they take a while to land, but once they land it is worth waiting and being patient. There are two ways to show how important it is to have patience, and one includes my favorite thing to do, which is hunting.

Colton Burg

Patience:
Patience is a guiding principle in the way I approach challenges and interactions. It's a tool I wield in various aspects of life. When faced with a difficult problem or complex task, I engage patience as a steady companion. Rather than rushing for a quick fix, I take the time to understand the nuances, breaking down the issue into manageable parts. This deliberate approach helps me navigate through the problem with a calm and composed mindset, seeking solutions that are well-thought-out and enduring.

In relationships, patience is an essential ingredient. I believe in allowing space for understanding and growth, acknowledging that everyone has their pace and perspective. Whether it's listening attentively to a friend in need or giving someone the time and support they require to overcome a challenge, patience enables me to provide genuine empathy and be a steady source of encouragement. It's about fostering connections built on understanding and trust, knowing that some bonds require nurturing and time to flourish.

Moreover, I use patience as a tool for personal development. It's the recognition that progress takes time and that setbacks are part of the journey. Patience allows me to embrace the process of self-improvement, whether it's learning a new skill, cultivating a habit, or pursuing a long-term goal. It's about celebrating small victories along the way and understanding that setbacks are opportunities to learn and grow stronger. Patience becomes the driving force behind perseverance, enabling me to stay committed to my aspirations even when the path ahead seems challenging.

Kayla Harris

Open-Mindedness:
Open-mindedness is a core value that resonates deeply with me. It's about being open to new concepts, viewpoints, and experiences without writing them off right away. Because it promotes development, empathy, and understanding in a diverse and ever-changing world, this value holds great significance for me.

Having an open mind has made it possible for me to accept many points of view. It's critical to recognize variety in today's globalized society and acknowledge that each person has a distinct history, values, and life experiences. I've been able to form deeper friendships and connections. For example, being in the midst of a difficult situation for a close friend was an experience that really brought home to me the value of empathy and open-mindedness. Contrary to what I had initially thought about how to help someone in these circumstances, I learned to realize that listening was simply ineffective by itself. It was a moment when my open-mindedness allowed me to empathize more deeply.

I always thought the greatest way to help was to offer suggestions or solutions. Still, I realized that sometimes just being there allows someone to express themselves without feeling pressured to provide a quick solution. As I sat with my friend and listened to her without throwing judgment, my relationship with my friend was strengthened and we were able to connect on a deeper level because of this change in perspective that came from having an open mind.

It helped me realize that being open-minded involves more than just embracing different points of view and looking into fresh concepts. It also involves acknowledging that everyone handles emotions differently, being flexible in our approach to relationships, and that, sometimes, closeness and silence speak louder than words of advice. This experience strengthened my belief that having an open mind can help people embrace different viewpoints and develop deeper connections by helping them empathize with others during their most vulnerable times.

Furthermore, being open-minded promotes personal development. It forces me to step outside of my comfort zone and challenges my limiting beliefs as well as new thoughts. It's simple to become mired in a pattern or believe that there's a single correct approach to accomplish tasks. But having an open mind helps me go beyond the box and find creative answers. This way of thinking has been especially beneficial for overcoming obstacles and addressing problems in both the personal and academic domains.

The fact that open-mindedness promotes empathy and understanding is another reason it is so important in my opinion. I'm more understanding of the perspectives and experiences of others when I have an open mind. It enables me to put myself in their position, appreciate their viewpoints, and handle circumstances with empathy. The aspect of being open-minded has had a big impact on how I interact with others and communicate, which has helped me create better, healthier connections.

Being open-minded, though, does not require blindly accepting everything without question. It's about keeping a healthy dose of skepticism and logical thinking while remaining open to new concepts. This balance makes sure that I consider new information carefully rather than taking it at face value.

All things considered, being open-minded is not only an advantage but also a compass that directs my actions in the world. I am inspired to approach life with curiosity, humility, and decency by it. This value's pillars—embracing different viewpoints, pursuing ongoing development, and encouraging empathy—all have a strong emotional connection for me and consistently guide my behavior.

LAWS OF LIFE

Amarion Dubose

Laws of Life are principles that determine individual moral value systems. These values are everyone's personal inventory of what we consider most important in life and can determine, to a great extent, character. Our character is defined by what we do, not what we say or believe. Everyone has a dream or goal they want to complete to succeed in life. The main idea of the Laws of Life is the brutal laws of nature in life. It's about the responsibilities and the actions that you've made. In the future, you could learn a life lesson from your mistakes because everyone makes mistakes. It's part of being human. That's what this example from Laws of Life means the most to me because I have made many honest mistakes and some mistakes that were somewhat crazy, but in the end, I have learned from them, and I'll look at them as a life lesson. I knew that one of life's lessons was to dream without fear. What would I do in a situation without failing? When I've made a mistake such as breaking or dropping anything, I would be scared to tell an adult about the accident due to how they may react, but being honest is the best thing to do, and I think it's responsible for owning up to the mistakes I've made. My parents, especially my dad, taught me how to be responsible. They reassured me to tell them if I ever have a problem. If not for them, I wouldn't have come this far in life at 18 years old.

Ella Hill

Empathy means a lot to me, especially as a particularly sensitive person. Empathy is connecting and understanding other people on a deep emotional level. All humans are inclined towards empathizing with others in their pain and suffering. It is the blueprint of all the good things we do. It's how we can connect with others.

Empathy is a strong emotion, I am a very empathetic person. When you see someone crying, you can feel it too. Whatever it is that caused their tears, you feel it too. That's empathy. And even if the emotions you're feeling weren't even what that person was experiencing, you still feel them just as strongly because that's how you imagined them to feel.

Empathy is a beautiful thing but is often seen as a weakness. Empathy is why I was never able to hunt. I have nothing against hunters, but I just can't do it myself. My dad's the same way. He cried when he shot a bird as a kid. It feels sad when you see roadkill or immediately feel your mood worsen when you notice someone else is sad. Empathy is understanding and feeling someone else emotions as if they're your own.

For me, empathy comes naturally, even when I don't want it there because I know it makes me seem really sensitive and weak sometimes. Society does the same with other values, such as kindness, though, so

I guess it doesn't really matter. I feel that all kids should be taught empathy if they don't already show signs of it.

Empathetic kids possess listening and understanding skills that allow them to thrive peacefully with classmates and other kids. A child who understands a concept has to put himself into the shoes of another who does not understand the same to transfer knowledge efficiently. Empathy is a very human thing, as in nature, you can never find animals showing empathy for each other. Without empathy, we wouldn't exactly be human.

Preston Irby

The core value that means the most to me is kindness. It is a way for people to show respect for one another. And why it means the most to me can be summarized with two words, "feels good". It always makes me feel good when I'm being kind to someone. For example, if I'm holding the door for someone, or something as simple as letting someone borrow my school laptop charger. It can never hurt a person to do something good for someone once in their life, even though it may be hard for some people to show kindness to others. When I think about kindness, I always come to a stopping point where little to no kindness is being shown to others in certain parts of social media. There are very few people being respectful to one another, yet so much bad stuff happening around us. And what do I say to that? I say we can push through all the bad stuff and just look on the bright side of things, even when it feels like there's no hope for it left. And just when we think we're losing sight of all the kindness in the world, just know that we can still be kind in many different ways, we just have to put some effort into it. In conclusion, what kindness means to me is how much it can impact a person in their life, it can even make someone's day just a little bit better.

Ana S. Montaño Alanis

I wish I had more imagination. Everyone seems to value imagination nowadays. I see it every time I'm online, with cool drawings or animations, or in comments of videos that seem to inspire thoughts and feelings from a brief song. Worlds created from a few instances seem to sprout from an infinite field of golden possibilities of what could be.

But it's suffocating. The sprouts are not sprouts any longer and they seem to have grown so, so high, and how can a tiny seed grow when there is no sunlight and there is no room to grow? And maybe those seeds were no good in the first place. We seem to value things that are cool and original, but seeds are seeds and all of them have been seeds so how could mine be any different from the ones already out there?

I wish I had more resilience. I'm not resilient. Or committed. I want to be. I want to be able to write constantly, and do well, and finish things that I never seem to finish, but then it grows too long. The goal is too far away. What good does it do to run when you don't see the finish line? You may be motivated when you start, but it gets harder to keep going. And before you know it you slow down and stop and realize that it was probably an impossible goal in the first place.

Because that's what the world says.

That it was always an unlikely goal and that the race wasn't even a proper path. And that even if you reach the goal, what would you accomplish? All the time running that race while running out of time to do things that matter more. Like money.

Money matters a lot. No matter what people say or movies tell you to believe, money is important. Your life is structured around it and it reflects on what you wear, what you eat, where you live, how you live, etc. So is it bad to already want to accommodate that way of thinking? To go into a job because I might be good at it but most importantly because they can pay me well? Yeah, maybe. My parents think so. They tell me to close my eyes and think of what I really want to be and there are two versions of me in that internal reflection reflecting off my eyes. In both I'm successful. In both, I seem happy (or am I trying to convince myself? I can't seem to discern that even now). But there is a definite difference in which I seem to be more proud of myself.

And I realize that I probably have selective hearing because I don't need more imagination and don't need better seeds. And that the only reason they didn't grow wasn't because I was telling them not to grow. Because I believed they couldn't grow. So I think I need to believe more. And maybe when it gets hard, I wish others would believe in me. To give me a little push so I can keep going. Because I want to keep growing. I don't think I've ever realized that so clearly before.

Colton Burg

One core value that resonates with me is empathy. It's the ability to understand and share the feelings of others, to walk in someone else's shoes without judgment or prejudice. Empathy forms the foundation of my interactions and shapes my worldview.

I believe empathy is crucial because it transcends boundaries, allowing connections with people from different backgrounds, cultures, and experiences. It opens opportunities to understand perspectives that might differ vastly from my own. In a world filled with complexities and oddities, empathy serves as a unifying force, fostering compassion and creating a sense of shared humanity.

Empathy isn't just about feeling sorry for someone or sympathizing with their plight. It's about actively listening, seeking to understand, and acknowledging the validity of another's emotions and experiences. It requires patience, an open mind, and a willingness to set aside previous notions.

This value has guided me in various aspects of life, from personal relationships to professional endeavors. In my interactions with friends, family, and colleagues, I strive to be present and attentive, offering support and understanding without assuming I try to comprehend their feelings. It's about creating a safe space for them to express themselves without fear of judgment.

Professionally, empathy plays a crucial role. As an older brother, understanding the needs and emotions of my siblings is essential in creating meaningful and impactful relationships. By putting myself in their shoes, I can understand their problems and help them out.

Moreover, empathy fosters a sense of social responsibility. It pushes me to advocate for those whose voices might be unheard. It fuels a desire to contribute positively to society, whether through volunteering, studying, or simply being a proper classmate for my peers.

At its core, empathy aligns with the concept of treating others as I'd like to be treated. It's about extending kindness, respect, and understanding, fostering an environment where everyone feels valued and seen. This value enriches my life by allowing me to forge deeper connections, learn from diverse perspectives, and contribute to a more compassionate and inclusive world.

In essence, empathy isn't just a value; it's a way of being a lens through which I perceive the world. It's not always easy; it requires emotional energy and a willingness to embrace vulnerability. But the rewards are immeasurable, as it enriches my life and the lives of those around me in ways that transcend boundaries and differences.

Zamiyah Rice

Creativity

I value all things in life, but creativity is one of the things I value the most. When I glance at the sky, I see many colors. They all blend in perfect harmony like a piece of art. That's what life is anyway: art.

By being alive, you shape and mold the world around you. We create things by having passions and thoughts. Every idea that you could think of, someone has already done it. But your individuality and uniqueness can never be copied or plagiarized.

When I draw, I often look at other people's art for inspiration. I've acknowledged that talent doesn't always equate to creativity. Knowing that it has helped me understand that my talent does not define my art. My art is sentimental to me, who I am is embedded within it. I appreciate others' creativity just as much as I appreciate my own.

To be human is to be creative. I see creativity in the way we socialize and talk. I see creativity in the way we think and the way we experience our lives. The industries that we have all come from a thought process, that someone had to create for it to exist.

Without creativity, there wouldn't be many special elements in life. There'd be no diversity and no individuality. Creativity is a salient character trait in my life. Not only does it inspire me, it makes living worth so much more. I soak up different ideas like a sponge, blending

WISDOM WRITERS:

and mixing them into something prepossessing.

Anonymous

Fairness means impartial and just treatment or behavior without favoritism or discrimination. When treated fairly, everyone works together, solves problems quickly, has fun, cares for one another, feels safe, and gets along. That is a way that many people want to live. It should be necessary for a person to act with fairness. If you do this, people will respect and trust you.

Not being treated fairly makes me feel like I'm not good enough. People who have any sort of authority should always show fairness. Here's an example: if you were playing a basketball game and were getting beat up on the court because the referees wouldn't call fouls, you would be mad. The result might be something that hurts you and your team.

I have experienced unfair situations during multiple basketball games my team and I have played. Away games are where this unfairness usually happens. The other teams seem like they purposely foul because they know there will be no consequences. We can barely touch our opponents and get a foul call because the referees want them to win so badly. Meanwhile, we're getting beat up and cheated out of a game.

Overall, I strongly dislike unfairness. People should always show fairness because all people have value. It is a core value that all people should have in their life. It is also important because it might lead to people resulting in an argument or even worse. Fairness should be shown no matter what power or authority you have.

Craig Ellington

Dedication

A character trait I would say I value in my daily life is dedication. With me being as busy as I am, I must stay dedicated to all the things I do to get everything done. Something I'm definitely dedicated to is basketball. I have to go to practice every day, which is three hours, which is a lot to do. If it is something you are not sure you are ready to do, you must know for sure because it takes away a lot of time. You also cannot let it overwhelm you when things get hard because they will. There is a lot that goes into basketball that a lot of people do not know, which is why it's a sport you are dedicated to. Basketball isn't the only thing I'm dedicated to in my life. I'm also dedicated to my schoolwork. As you get older your schoolwork will get harder and you will have to put more effort into it than you think. Being dedicated to school work is also staying on top of your grades, which means you must ask questions and see what extra things you can do, which is a little more than the average high schooler. I'm also dedicated to my job. Being as much of a busy person as I am, I must stay dedicated to all the things I do. When it's cold outside or just simply working under hard conditions, I understood when I got the job that I made a commitment and must be able to handle the situation. This is why I think a trait I value the most is dedication because of all the hardships I endure on a daily basis.

Anonymous

I use honesty in my everyday life. Sometimes, people think I'm too honest. They would give me a stank face if they took what I said the wrong way when I was being completely honest. Being completely real with people can sometimes be hard because some people are sensitive. Sometimes, being honest can hurt people's feelings because you never know what's going on in someone's life. People may take being honest wrong or take it to heart. I love being honest when people ask me my opinion on things. Giving someone your opinion on a situation can be helpful to some people, but some people don't want your opinion, and they feel disrespected when you are trying to help them.

Honesty plays a big role because my little sister looks up to me. When my sister gets older, I don't want her to do anything she regrets, so I will be honest about everything she does. I will be there for my sister anytime she needs something or someone to talk to. When my sister gets to high school, and she asks me if I have done this, I will tell her what to do if it happens to her in high school. I want my sister to be better than me. I want her to follow her dreams and go to college. I just want my sister to be a good person in life. My mom always tells me if I tell the truth, the outcome won't be as bad as if I would lie. Also, having someone you trust can help you be honest with people. Gain someone's trust that you can be 110% honest with them without them getting mad or offended.

Kareem Elnaham

Humbleness

I think an important core value in life is being humble. Don't take everything for granted. Everything could change in just a day. If you worked hard for everything always remember where you came from and how it all started. I'm saying don't think you are better than anyone if you don't know what they do and what happens to them. Don't make fun of people because they don't have the same clothes or expensive shoes. An example of this is Lionel Messi. Even if he is the best player and won the most trophies he doesn't go bragging about how good he is. He still thinks he isn't the best and he is kind to every team he plays against. A lot of people need to make this a main core value. Now, you have people on Instagram flexing off their money, making fun of people who don't have as much money. Don't get me wrong, if they worked for that money I'm happy for them. However, I don't think it is good to show it off and make people feel bad about it. Being humble can come with benefits. People could talk to you more about their problems. It will create loyalty between friends and family. People will look at you in a good way. And being humble will motivate you to do good things for other people, like giving people food when they don't have it or helping your friend with personal problems. This is why I think being humble is important.

Madison Love

Integrity is a characteristic that many of us value in ourselves, and it's one we look for consistently in our leaders. But what does it really mean to have integrity? Integrity is defined as the quality of being honest and having strong moral principles; moral uprightness, the state of being whole and undivided, and/or a sound, unimpaired or perfect condition. You could say that integrity is always doing the right thing, even when no one is looking, or when the choice isn't easy. You might see integrity as staying truthful to yourself and others around you, even when faced with the consequences of the choices that you make.

I think of integrity as being honest, trustworthy, fair, responsible, caring, and having the moral courage to do the right thing. Without it, we as individuals will fall short of realizing our full potential. When we live our lives with integrity we let our actions speak for who we are and what we believe in. Integrity is a choice we make, and it's a choice we must keep making, every moment of our lives. There are several reasons why integrity is so important. When we have integrity we're dependable, and, when we hold ourselves accountable for our actions, we become role models for others to follow.

Zy'Keria Long

Generosity! Sharing, caring, giving, and being nice. You don't know what other people are dealing with. Being nice is something I adore. God will bless you if you are generous. Being kind to others is something that goes a long way in life. I'm always kind to other people because it is just right. I show generosity by giving to others and being there for others. As someone who grew up receiving a lot of things, giving is something I'm passionate about. I've earned an award from one of my teachers Mrs. Allen. On the award paper, Mrs. Allen said I always say kind words and give her hugs. She has shown a lot of generosity to me by also helping me and keeping me motivated throughout the day. I show generosity by showing others that I care about them just by telling these people they look good or telling the girls they are so pretty. Being a generous person is being friendly, being nice. Generous people are the people who can light up a room when they walk in. When you are generous with your time and with your attention to your resources and you are generous with other people, you can light up a room. You can light up someone's family. You can light up your workplace. You can light up the people you work around. With your generosity, you can light up the world. People think that to be generous, you'll have to have to give more but that's not the key. As a very generous person, I appreciate what I have and I appreciate what others give to me. As a generous person, I don't feel entitled to anything. The Bible says to be generous 1 Timothy 6:17-19 commands them to do good, to be rich in good deeds, and to be generous and willing to share. Generosity is a simple act of kindness.

Hannah Price

Life is hard without having grit. Without grit, you can give up so easily. Like me, I take a very challenging class the class is EKG, which is a health class that kind of focuses on your heart. You run EKGS on your classmates. Although I wanted to stop taking that class, I will tell you why I wanted to stop. It was because I didn't believe in myself, and that I could take a class like that. I thought I couldn't catch up and that I would be behind, but I had to believe in myself. Nurse Jenny believed in me and told me I could do it. Also, I thought I wouldn't pass any of the tests she gave us. I thought I wouldn't get it. I had to tell myself I could push through it and that I could do it. Now, I study hard for each test and study more. Now, I'm taking a dual enrollment class. Plus, I'm doing clinics. I do all three by having grit, believing in myself, and pushing myself to achieve all I can do. It was just the same with AHEC. I thought I couldn't do it either. I had to tell myself again that all that "can't" is not in my vocabulary anymore, and that I can't say it anymore. I'm doing well in both courses. I go to clinics in February and March and I'm very excited. I want to see how good I will do. I pray I do well. I have the grit to go there and have a good mindset.

Addyson Tillman

Honesty. Integrity. Those two are hard to tell apart, at least personally for me. I would love to be able to say that I can tell the difference between them, but not really, even with googling the difference. Still, even if I cannot tell the difference *that* well, I need to work on *both* of them. I need to start being honest to myself about what I want to do – I need to just latch onto a goal, and for honesty? Honesty is hard. Difficult. I feel a little silly for saying this, but I cannot go a *day* without lying. Be it to my friend about a small, little thought, I lie about things to make it sound better. Even in a huge problem where I have to make the lie actually sound believable, I still *lie*. That is the problem with me – I *am* a problem. It always goes unnoticed, though. One day I *know* my lies are gonna catch up to me. I dread the day when it happens, I really do. It will bite me back, and I know I will be like a dog on the street when it does: utterly helpless. And staying true to myself? It just cannot happen. I just do not stand up for what I believe in, or latch onto something, like a goal or such. I am not the kind of person that I should be. But if you want my honesty in this? I am fine with being like this. There is my honesty. I should not be that happy about it, yet I am somewhat content with it. Integrity, like I said, is difficult for me, and I do sometimes wish I could change. Maybe all the time, whilst still being content with being a lying machine. It is bad.

Tamaya Tolliver

The Value of Respect

Respect has different meanings to people. It can mean to admire someone through their abilities or qualities. It could also mean agreeing with someone without being detrimental. It builds trust in your relationship with family, friends, peers, etc. It teaches you humility and responsiveness.

I value respect because you can go a long way with this trait. From the day you learn your first word to the day you die, you will learn respect throughout your lifetime. It can be shown by listening to adults, offering constructive criticism, accepting someone's faults, and other ways. Even something like a smile can be a sign of respect. There are so many ways to give respect that you can't name them all.

When I was younger, I used to live with my grandparents up until the day I went to live with my mother. During that time, I learned different traits from my grandma, respect being the most important. Since she was a Christian, one of the Ten Commandments she practiced the most in my childhood was "Honor thy father and thy mother, that your days may be long upon the land which the Lord your God is giving you." (Exodus 20:12 KJV). She taught me to treat people how I want to be treated. It was a powerful lesson because it taught me to be compassionate and considerate towards others. My family showed me how to respect people and vice versa. As Proverbs 22:6 states in the Bible, "Train up a child in the way he should go: and when he is old, he will not depart from it."

Jamiya Jenkins

We all make mistakes when we are doing the wrong thing. People make mistakes when they tell people to do something stupid. You make mistakes when you fix something on a car or something in somebody's house. You make mistakes when you fuss at somebody who didn't do it. You make mistakes when you put the wrong seasoning in a food thing you are making. People make mistakes when they make the wrong order for somebody. People make mistakes when they mess up on a project they did. You make mistakes when bullying somebody who doesn't do anything to you. You make mistakes when you are not being respectful to a teacher or anyone you are around. You make mistakes when you are not being nice to somebody. People make mistakes when they do nasty things or fight in front of kids. You make mistakes when you put random stuff on a test when you don't know the answer. You make mistakes when you forget to study, and you have to take a test.

People make mistakes when treating others wrongly in a relationship. When you play football, and you throw a ball, and they don't catch it, that can be a mistake. You will make mistakes when you play basketball. People make mistakes when they get the ball taken from them. People make mistakes when they double-travel or carry. You make mistakes when you foul out the game. Refs make mistakes when they make stupid calls. They make mistakes when they don't do the right thing. You make mistakes when you bump into people walking in the mall or somewhere. You make mistakes when you say bad words in front of teachers or people around you. When I make mistakes, I try to learn from them. Everyone makes mistakes, but not everyone accepts responsibility and tries to correct their mistakes. More people should be willing to accept responsibility, learn from mistakes, and move forward instead of looking backward.

Mathew Kendrick

Respect Is a Given

"Respect is earned!" "No, respect is given!" Whichever side of the argument you fall on, we can all agree that respect is important. I, however, believe that respect is something more than other people, something bigger than words, bows, or other made-up pleasantries. Respect is who you are. It is all the actions you take and all the thoughts you believe. When you respect the people, places, and all things around you, that reflects the very constitution of your soul.

It is most certainly not easy. Not a day passes that does not tempt me to revert back to the primitive state of lacking respect. Not a day passes that I do not fail in some regard. After all, I, you, and everyone else are only human. But humanity is the ultimate goal, the product of respect. Respect separates us from the animals that fight, kill, and desecrate. They have no sense of empathy or purity, they lack the respect that we have. That is not to say there is no goodness in animals, but they are not endowed by the Creator with the same qualities as we are.

He made us different from the rest, in His image, but flawed. It is in my nature to abandon respect, but with the gift He gave me, I can will myself to greatness. He was the best of us but suffered and died like the worst of us in order to save us. That action is the pinnacle of respect. They are similar, salvation and respect, not only in the sense that they come from the same giver. They both are given, whether the receiver will accept or not. There is no hope in trying to earn either one. Speaking for myself, my wrongs always outweigh my rights. I "deserve" no salvation, no respect, right?

I do not believe in "deserve". It is a concept that is entirely manmade, artificial, plastic. Did we deserve for a man, a God no less, to be tortured to death for us? Of course not, just as no other person deserves our respect, but we give it anyway. The same can be said for the negative. Someone disrespects me so does he deserve for me to disrespect him? I believe he still is given respect. Two wrongs never make a right, contrary to the ancient belief of Hammurabi. Mahatma Gandhi famously spoke against this, "An eye for an eye leaves the whole world blind."

He should still have my respect, not "even," but especially if his actions show a lack of respect for me. I would like myself to show kindness to him who would not show me the same. That is not to say that there should be no consequences for disrespectful actions. If he breaks a law against me, he should be arrested. This is not an act of revenge but a prevention to protect those who would follow me. I will not become the man who disrespects me, because respect is a given.

DEAR 7TH GRADE SELF

Amarion Dubose

Dear 7th self,

I know that I was young and I really hesitated to own up to the honest mistakes I made in the past. Besides the mistakes, 7th Grade was the craziest school year I've experienced in just middle school, but thankfully my parents helped me through that year until we left and transferred to UCS. Ever since I was 12 years old, I was always imagining the possibility of all my dreams coming true. As 5 years have passed, now about to graduate from high school, I kinda figured out what type of person I am. I would describe myself as an optimist and driven person, who dreams about great things, and actually trying to figure out how to make those dreams happen in reality. Another thing I did learn is that nothing has really changed about me. I get really excited and a little impatient when an event or a party is coming up. To this day, when I'm myself, I would just think about what event is coming up, and what I can do to make it better. In 7th grade, I came up with a big event of turning my grandmother's house into a Disneyland, due to the fact how big her yard is. Now I look back at that idea, and think that was the best idea I ever came up with, but now I realized that it was impossible for that to happen and it was all just a fairytale. Right now, the only thing I dream and wish for is things that I can make happen in reality.

Zy'Kirea Long

Dear 7th grade self
　　　　Hello there, are you good? You are in the 11th grade now and you've learned a lot about yourself, from other people and things you didn't even know about. I wish I could've told you to just slow down, and take a break. I wish I could have told you to take breaks for yourself. You've learned that you are a smart person and a caring and loving person. You have come to be the sweetest person ever. Now you came up to be HSP (Highly Sensitive Person), but that's your business as Tabitha Brown would say. As you became a high school student, you were in the worst state possible. You took your anger out on someone who now stands to help you the most (Thank You, Mrs. Allen). It caused you damage but you learned your lesson and formed a vision and passion for yourself. You once wanted to help others feel and see that something can change and be different. Because it is possible.

Zamiyah Rice

Dear younger me,

I've spent a lot of time rebuilding my character. I'm tough on myself when it comes to how I present myself, how I talk, and how other people see me. It becomes obsessive and tiring. Younger me, I want to let you know that it's okay. Who you are isn't perfect and that's completely fine. There's going to be times where you screw up and make bad choices. You're a kid, so don't expect yourself to know most things. Being the bigger person in every situation isn't possible. You let your emotions get the best of you sometimes and that's completely human. Mistakes are made because you're meant to learn from them.

I want you to keep trying and pursue whatever you want to pursue. You're strong-minded, creative, talented, and beautiful. You have your beliefs set and that's amazing. There's more rough times coming along the way but you know that you– well, we–will push through no matter what.

I've always admired your originality and thinking skills. You might not know this yet, but you're smart and brave. You've always been a lovable human being. I hope that we both take that to heart and realize it. I always say: "Things can only get worse," but I know that's far from

the truth. So far, we've improved a great amount over just three years. I expect and know that greater things will come out of us.
   I'm proud of you.

Sincerely,
   Older you.

Matthew Buck

Dear 7th grade self,

 Hello, this is you from the future. I'm going to tell you what to be prepared for and how. People are still going to be the same. School will get harder. You will have to deal with some people who will try to get you to do the wrong things. DON'T DO THEM!! You will face some bad consequences. Life will get harder, too. You will have to prepare to step up around other people. You will have more responsibilities like driving and caring for family and pets. You will have to do the right things like study for every type of test. You will not be able to play sports in the 9th grade because you didn't take math seriously.

 Sometimes, your friends might bring you down, get you in trouble, or just make you mad, but try not to show any emotion because that's what they want. You will have to stand up for yourself because, if you don't, people will use that to their advantage. You will have to use the time you have to do work. If you have homework, you should do it as soon as you have free time so you have more time to play video games or go outside. You will have to help out with your family because some will have some bad surgery or they are just getting older in life. You will also have to prepare for the loss of a pet. See ya.

 Sincerely,
 Matthew Buck

James Edmonds

Dear 7th grade self,

I am going to let you know how my life is in 9th grade at age 14. This year is my first semester, and I had all A's. I will talk about sports now because there is not much to talk about in school. I play football, and I did not make the baseball team. This did not bother me too much because I like football a lot. I even got in on a few plays in varsity football. I am encouraging you to eat more protein and stay healthy. This past summer, I have two personal lawns, and I work for my father. This coming season, I plan on buying half of the lawn care business and getting all the money from all the lawns. This past year, my favorite thing to do was duck hunting. I got a new Benelli Super Black Eagle 3. I have also gotten a lot of other new duck hunting stuff. This past Christmas break, I went on a duck hunting trip to Texas. When I went to Texas, I killed a lot of ducks. Another thing I have started doing a lot more that I enjoy is deer hunting. The past Christmas, I got a Beretta 308, with Leopold scope. Another thing I still like doing is riding four-wheelers. In fact, with the money I have made from grass cutting, I bought a four-wheeler. The four-wheeler I bought was a Honda 300.

Sincerely,
James Edmonds, 9th grade year

Craig Ellington

Dear 7th-grade self,

    This is where your life will start moving fast. You will start experiencing more things and being exposed to a lot more. Take everything slowly and don't rush anything. Don't take anything for granted because you will see that time flies by. As you make decisions, think about how they are going to affect you in the future. Try to participate in any and everything you can because those memories will be things you will hold on to for the rest of your life. Don't move too fast, and don't be in a rush to be older, be in a higher grade level, or even things such as getting your driver's license. A lot of things will take you by surprise, so just handle those situations the best way you can. Also, don't retaliate to most situations based on your initial instinct. If there is time, quickly think about the best way to handle that situation. Take all your grades and classes seriously, even the ones you may think won't matter. In the end, they most likely will. Take the ACT as many times as possible. You may think that you do not need to because you are only in the seventh grade, but the more you take and are familiar with it, the better you will do as you get older. Doing this may be able to help you get a scholarship to a school or be easily accepted by others with a high composite score. All this information that I'm giving you will be so helpful, so don't take it for granted.

WISDOM WRITERS:

Sincerely,
Craig Ellington

Anonymous

Dear 7th grade self,
    You probably didn't expect to play football, but we ended up playing it and liking it a lot. We started taking school more seriously and making more money. Our brother got us a PS5. You have new friends and got close to people you wouldn't have thought you would. We started weightlifting and trying to get bigger. We started driving. You need to focus more on school and stop acting like it won't matter. You will meet some people that will cause you some problems, but don't think about it too much. You're going to go back to Yemen and meet your grandma again after 6 years of not seeing her, and meet some of your cousins and make some friends there. You're going to see your childhood friend again. Then, you are going to go to Turkey and have a lot of fun over there. The bad part is you will lose a lot of weight, but we didn't give up. We started gaining more weight and weight lifting even more than before. Then, we sign up for football again after being gone for so long. We didn't get as much playtime as we had last year, but we don't give up. We have to understand we were bigger last season by the next season we will be bigger. Your little brother also got bigger. That is basically everything that has happened so far. We are in our first year of high school and everything so far is going smoothly.

Gradon Fike

Dear 7th grader Gradon,

Hello, it's me, the older you. It's quite the rocky road ahead, little one. We never did move, by the way. We're still here at UCS, but we are in a new building which is pretty cool. It's the most expensive school I've ever been in, like, ever. Trust me, it does get better after seventh grade. Everyone stops talking about you, and all they do now is tolerate you. They don't talk to you nearly as much because there are always five or ten people in the vicinity. By the way, you will have the same teachers until you get to ninth grade. They like me, which isn't really that bad. I mean, you will miss them and all, but they will still be there teaching different and younger classes. I think we might see them next year in tenth grade, but I have no idea.

There will be a class that you don't really like and that will be Mrs. Tolliver's math class. No offense! You don't really like math that much. By the way, you will get very low grades to the point you're barely passing. 70s and 60s are all we will get for this year, with Mrs. Tolliver's class being the lowest grade for us, which is unfortunate. Work harder to try to pass math with at least an 80! But yeah, that's pretty much how your year will go, and also, you will love having Mr. Russell and Mr. Daniels as your teachers. They're pretty cool dudes. Keep in check.

Yours, well… Us truly

Gradon Haggard Fike

Anonymous

Dear 7th grade self,
    I'm glad to be writing you. There is so much that I've learned since your time that I think you will benefit from. I've learned a lot in school, of course, but it's not just book smarts that I've improved in. School will get harder, and you'll have to allocate more time to solely doing school work, but you won't have so much of a problem with that. What I really need you to understand is that you need to be more careful. In your actions and your words, you need to put careful thought into the implications that they will have today, tomorrow, and a year from now. I know for a fact that you won't like hearing this, but if you want to be better off, you're going to have to do this for the rest of your life. Sometimes, maybe even most of the time, you can say things that hurt others. This might come as a shock to you, but I have to let you know that you're not a very good person. It's not the end of the world, though, because you will come to realize very soon that no one is a truly good person. A lot of people will judge you, and a lot of people will love you. What you need to know is that people don't judge based on how good you are, because no one is. They judge based on the amount of effort you put towards being good; that's what counts. You're going to have to work on that effort part, and please don't make jokes at the expense of others; they're not funny.
    Sincerely,

ANONYMOUS

Your future self
P. S. Go outside, boy. You're too pale.

Ryan Vaughan

Dear 7th grade Ryan Vaughan,

    Hello, this is you from the future. I am in the ninth grade and I would like to give you some advice for the coming years. The first thing is to always do your homework, or you will get behind. Another thing is to not use sports as an excuse for missing homework. You can get in a lot of trouble doing that because, most of the time, practice ends at 5:30, giving you enough time to finish your homework. Another way is to not be depressed because you are not the most popular. If anything, if you are popular, it distracts you from your school work and will most likely keep you from being academically successful.

    In 8th grade, you will pass with no trouble and become a starter in middle school football. You get an Oculus for your birthday and then go to Mexico with your family. Later, you will go to Hype, play with your friends, beat them in laser tag, and eat at the Mexican restaurant. You were doing way better this time in summer workouts than you did last year. You hit 245 pounds on squats, 135 power clean, and 115 on the bench. You did not get as tired as you did last year running. These are some sneak peeks on what going to happen in the future.

    Sincerely,
    9th grade Ryan Vaughan

Madison Love

Dear Madison,
 Hey there! It's me, your future self. I'm a senior now. Yeah, I'm shocked that I made it, too. I thought, by now, I would have dropped out, but we pushed through. The advice I would like to give you is not to be afraid to voice your opinions and advocate for yourself. I would encourage myself to be more open to conversations with people I don't usually converse with. I would push myself to work harder and not give up when times get rough.
 Sincerely,
 Madison

Anonymous

Dear 7th Grade Self,
    Your first year in middle school will be hard. Give it everything you've got. If you do not know it, ask your teacher for help. I know you don't remember a lot from 6th grade. You can write down notes to help you understand what the teacher is trying to say. Don't be afraid to ask a friend for help. It wouldn't hurt to ask if you need help. Your friend should be nice enough to help you if you've helped them in the past. Studying for your tests will help you. Study for at least 15-30 minutes each night. Do your homework and keep your grades up. Don't let what other people think or say dictate you and your choices. Don't let other people bring you down.

  Pick your friends wisely, and do not be around people who get in trouble a lot. Try to pick friends who are quiet and calm. Being around people who are getting in trouble every day aren't good people to be around. If they get in trouble, and even if you have nothing to do with them getting in trouble, you and your whole friend group most likely will get in trouble because you're guilty by association. If they are troublemakers and class clowns, keep your distance, because you will eventually get used to being around their foolishness. You will start to act like them and become a troublemaker with them.

  This is the year you start playing sports and being in athletic P.E. The first year in athletic P.E. will be hard because you aren't used to running and lifting weights. Yes, people are going to think you run slow or you are weak. In your first year playing a sport, you probably will not know anything about this sport. People are going to think you suck, but that's when you show them you can do it better than they can because you put in the work to get better at the sport. During your off-season, work on getting better and learning more about this sport so next season, you can come back harder, stronger, and even better.

Work hard and play and hard,
Anonymous

Anonymous

Dear 7th grade self,
 Are you okay? Be honest. Because for us, it gets better. Sure, we have our moments where we are not okay. But I promise it gets better. I understand why you are not happy. I mean, when I transferred – yes, you get to leave that "school" – I was way happier. Apart from the fact that we still have to go through some ups and downs with our family, which definitely won't change now, you'll get happier. You will also meet the girl that you will just immediately click with. Okay, not immediately. Give it a month or so. But aside from moving to a new school, I do not really have advice. I mean, we are a loner at that school, are we not? People won't start seeing you as cool or anything if you do try something. I know you already know this, but people are interested in our brother more than us at that school. I hate it, and I know for a fact you do too. It is hard to be happy in that place when you have nobody there for you or accepting of you. Also, be careful on Valentine's Day, or just keep quiet when your teacher asks a question. I learned the hard way that our childhood friend was the one to hurt us the most after that day. But I hate that school and the people there. They do not do any good for us. I hated how my brother was just the beauty of the school. It makes you feel inferior. Which is what everyone sees you as, by the way. Inferior. You are not really a friend to them… You are just there. Inferior and

ANONYMOUS

there.
  Sincerely,
  Your older self

SPORTS

Yazmine McAboy

I will always remember basketball playoffs day because it was my first year playing varsity. We had to play our regular season of around 19 games and win an area tournament. We played Keith High School, beat them in the area tournament 1st, and then lost to A.L. Johnson. Despite this loss, we were the area runner-up. We still went to playoffs in Montgomery, AL in February 2023. I was an 8th grader with only one year of experience and was able to assist my team in making the playoffs.

We practiced and worked hard daily to get a spot in the playoffs. During the summer, we would have 2-hour practices and three games to prepare us for the season. My family had to buy my warm-up clothing and my shoes. As an 8th grader, it was challenging to keep my grades up because I was more focused on sports than my class work. I would sit in class and watch films all day. At playoffs, it was hard because we weren't scoring very much. We were in our heads about the game, but we kept fighting until the end. We lost, but that doesn't stop us from trying to make it again the next year.

In the hotel, everyone had roommates. When we settled in, everybody entered the coach's room, played games, and ate snacks for about 30-45 minutes. Some games we played were uno and spoon. Some snacks we had were fruit snacks, apples, and oranges. After we were done playing, we went into our rooms, chilled, and talked to each other until the coach texted everyone and said it was time to go to bed and get ready for the game the next day.

The next day was game day, a very important day. Everyone got dressed and went down to eat breakfast because we had to leave and go to the arena because we had to play at 11:00. After the first team played, we went to the locker room and got ready to play. We played Loachapoka High School. We were down at least 2-5 points throughout the whole game, but toward the end, we fouled them, and they beat us by 7.

The biggest influence on me in sports is Javionna Harrison. She encourages me to keep going even when I don't want to or about to give up. Honestly, I don't know what I will do when she graduates. Coach K. Lewis always encourages me to keep going. I am thankful for them in my life. I would advise other athletes to focus on their school work first, then focus on their sport. To get scholarships, you must have a good GPA/ good grades. I enjoyed playing basketball throughout middle school and will continue playing throughout my high school years. - **Yazmine McAboy**

NARRATIVE 4 EXPERIENCE

Narrative 4 is a global network of students, educators, and artists who use empathy-based storytelling to equip individuals with the emotional and practical skills they need to help bridge divides between and within communities. Leslie Gibbs, our Director of Instructional Support, emailed our teacher over the summer and shared a Narrative 4 interview clip from The Today Show. Mrs. Allen connected with a regional coordinator for Narrative 4 and completed training to become a facilitator.

Avery Long

Narrative 4 is when two people exchange each other's stories and tell them to others out loud but in the person's shoes as it happened. The purpose of Narrative 4 is to build empathy between others, teach compassion and leadership, and develop emotional and practical skills, as well as imagination and deep listening.

My experience with Narrative 4 was awesome. At first, I was very hesitant when Mrs. Allen asked me and Angel to be the first ones to try it out at UCS. It was kind of scary because I didn't really know Angel, and I was not a good public speaker. We both agreed to try it out and went to the conference room to tell each other our story. Mrs. Allen had given us a few prompts to choose from, so it wasn't very hard to choose. We both chose to talk about an unfamiliar place. I had told Angel my story, which was about coming to UCS for the first time. As I talked, we walked through my story together. She had realized quickly that we were both going to have similar stories.

Angel told me her story after I finished, and she was talking about her first time at UCS. Angel came to UCS this year and quickly became comfortable and felt at home. Before coming to UCS, Angel was scared about friend groups and wanted to feel included. She had already met a few people but wanted to make sure she wouldn't be a burden when joining groups. This year, on the first day, she walked in. A few people were yelling and screaming, saying "It's a new girl" "I hope she's in our class" "Hey, hey, what's your name". Angel said she didn't know how to feel until she realized she was in their homeroom. They were so excited about her being there. Angel quickly made new friendships here at UCS. She felt comfortable and at home. She mentioned how, before coming to UCS, she told herself it's okay to not have friends or a friend group. As she talked to me more, she told me she came here to learn and to grow and develop for her future. I quickly noticed how Angel and I were the same. We were both nervous about coming to a new school, we were both at peace if we didn't click in friend groups, and we both went to school to learn and not socialize.

In the end, I loved getting to talk to Angel and learn more about her. We found out we have a lot more in common than we realize. After talking, we went back to class and re-told each other's story as if we were them. It was hard remembering details, but getting to put yourself in their shoes helps you imagine what they went through. Simply getting to learn more about others is the best thing to do. At school, we see each other and maybe say hey and "talk" to one another, but do we really know each other? This project helped me understand and learn more about Angel. I hope in the future, this project brings us closer together.

Kayla Harris

I liked getting to know others and about portions of their life. I didn't like having to speak in front of the class, though. I have mixed emotions about Story Exchange. I feel like it should continue, but most students probably aren't comfortable sharing their personal experiences with other students. They may feel uncomfortable with the reactions of their classmates. I would recommend the Story Exchange to other students. There are plenty of students out there who would love and learn from an experience like this. I think I was a little nervous beforehand. During the exchange, I was much more nervous because I was afraid of their reaction, and I felt like I needed to withhold a lot of information out of habit.

Angel Burrell

What I liked about this experience was Avery and I had a lot in common. Avery is very relatable and easy to talk with. We should do the Story Exchange more often because we will learn more about our classmates. Also, we will find out if we have more things in common. I would recommend this process because it makes you come out of your shell and comfort zone. Before I started talking to Avery, I was very nervous. During the situation, I was getting more comfortable in the setting. After the exchange, I felt more comfortable around her since she was easy to relate to. I think this process would be helpful in Morning Meetings. It would be beneficial because it would help students better their socialization skills.

POSITIVE AND NEGATIVE ASPECTS OF HIGH SCHOOL

Amarion Dubose

The only positive aspect of high school is being a senior. When you're a senior in high school, you can start preparing your life, and what you want to major in. Right now, I'm currently in the 12th grade and graduation is coming up soon. As I'm getting ready for graduation, I have a checklist of things that I need in the last remaining months of high school. On February 10, I'm taking the ACT Test so I can get into Meridian Community College in Fall 2024. March 21 will be my last day being an employee at the local grocery store, because the majority of my senior year, especially 1st Semester, I've been pretty busy with school, football, and having a job at the exact same time, and barely had any time to relax. So, I have decided to spend the rest of my high school to focus on school, applying for better jobs, and doing things I love to do outside of school until I get hired at Walmart or Books-A-Million.

The negative aspect of high school is that I have sort of overloaded myself. As I mentioned before, my senior year was pretty busy; it was mainly the 1st semester. I was on the UCS football team and had a job while focusing on school. I wouldn't want anyone to go through that much stress when they are about to come out of high. On the football team, we would have football every week from August until the season ends in November. But the hardest part about it is that during the school weeks, we practiced Mondays-Thursdays and game day was on Fridays and the weekends, I had to go straight to work.

James Edmonds

Positive

A positive aspect of being my age is being able to be more independent. This is a positive thing for 2 reasons. The first is being able to make money, and the other is being able to do more things. The reason I like to make money is so I can buy more things I want. The other thing I can do with this money is make my grass-cutting business larger and on a bigger scale. The reason I like doing more things is because that falls in the category of me hanging out with my friends.

Negative

The negative part of me being my age is having to be more responsible and independent. The negative part of having to be more responsible is I have to always make sure I always make good decisions. So if I am with my friends, and I wonder if I should do something, I go ahead and tell myself no. The negative part of having to be independent is I have to pay for more of my meals when I go out on my own. The other negative part of being independent is I have to buy my own clothes and personal things more often.

Kareem Elnaham

One positive thing about high school is how much fun you will have. You will always have fun in any type of way. You could have fun playing sports, hanging out with friends, and learning new things. Even weight lifting, if you're an athlete.

One negative thing, I would say, is all the work you get. There are due dates and you get a ton of assignments. It will stress you out at least a few times. He loses track of time and the next thing you know you have 3 assignments due tomorrow, and you have a test to study for.

Jamiya Jenkins

Things that I like about my age are that you get to drive your own car. You can go out and have fun with your friends. You can go out in public and meet new people. You can help other people out in the neighborhood and help the elderly. You could learn how to do things like braid hair, do nails, do makeup and other things. You can get a job till you get old enough to do what you wanna do.

The thing I don't like about high school is that you have to do a lot of work. You have to go to a lot of classes. High school can be very stressful and frustrating. Some of these teachers don't have respect. They have middle schoolers and high schoolers together and the hallways are crowded. We don't go on field trips that much.

Mathew Kendrick

Sometimes I feel like there is nothing good about being the age that I am, but that's not true; there is always a silver lining to every cloud. Whenever I feel like I take too much for granted, I remember that while I am young, I am free. I am not burdened by the growing responsibilities of maturity. Even though I still feel the looming responsibility over my head, I know that it waits for me patiently until I am old enough to handle it. Not to imply that I have no responsibilities. I still have to keep my grades up, my room clean, and my cats alive. It's just that the Lord has yet to give me something I can't handle, and I doubt He ever will.

Reflecting upon my list of woes and worries, it can be challenging to pick one that stands out above the others. If I had to pick one negative aspect of being my age, it would be that I am in the uncomfortable transitioning phase between childhood and adulthood. It feels like I was a kid yesterday, and I will be an adult tomorrow. I feel like I missed out on important experiences of yesterday. I feel like today will not prepare me for tomorrow, and I will miss out on more key experiences. All my peers are leaving me behind, but time still marches forward for all of us at the same pace, demanding the same of us as we go regardless of the past.

Yazmine McAboy

Being in high school is hard, especially the first semester. As a freshman, you have to stay on top of your work and use time management early because it gets harder as you go to the next grade. Once you get through the first semester, everything goes by smoothly. Doing all your assignments and paying attention in class will be helpful when it comes down to the tests. Everything you do in class or on assignments will be the same thing on the test. If you fail a test, your grade will drop really low and it will be hard to pull it back up, so I suggest studying for your test. That way, you could have a decent grade.

In high school, there are going to be people who talk about you, but don't let that affect you. Focus on yourself and your grades. Your main focus should be yourself. Don't worry about others. If someone bullies you, you will have people who will have your back. They might not be your friend but they will stand up for you. Some days, your friends might have a bad morning and just dislike everyone that day or don't want to talk. Don't force them. Just give them their space and let them come talk to you when they are ready. Always remember that as a high school student, you treat everyone how you would want to be treated because in high school, people are mean and hateful so try to be nice to everyone.

Zamiyah Rice

One positive thing about being in high school at the age of 15 is that I have two more years until freedom. I wouldn't say absolute freedom, but the fact that I made it through hell. High school for me is the absolute worst, it adds to my existing problems. Getting it off my back would be a breath of fresh air. One negative thing that I can think of is the people that I am surrounded each day. I get tired of seeing the same people and hearing them talk and interact with each other, they irk me.

Addyson Tillman

A positive thing about being my age is that I get to drive soon! I am currently fourteen years old and I will be going on fifteen in July. I have only five months left to wait until I can drive with an adult! It makes me excited to know I will finally be able to call the car I am paying off with my money mine. We got it back in September when we were in Daphne. We got it in during our beach trip. I love to drive that car. But a negative aspect about being my age is also that adults do not seem to understand things. Yeah, I am still a child, but I am growing. I expect them to understand that I am just basically a ball of hormones. I am gonna be moody, rude, and the farthest thing from obedient. I understand, though. It is hard to deal with me, and... Yeah. That is also kind of a me problem. But again, they were a kid once, so why do they not get it? I just do not get it. Anyway, those are my aspects of it!

Tamya Tolliver

I've been at the University Charter School since the beginning of the first year. I was one of the first students to make history. I was in the 7th grade when I came here, and I am currently a senior. Since then, I've had positive and negative aspects of my school. Don't get me wrong, I love being here, but there are some things that I wish were different. I'll talk about the positive aspects first.

One positive aspect is that UCS provides opportunities for students to advance their learning and gain work-based experience. Most of our projects are student-led and place-based: BrewCS, Wisdom Writers, DIVEs, etc. I think that it's a unique way to let students show their leadership skills. It prepares us for our future. Another aspect is dual enrollment. Dual enrollment is the number of college classes you take during high school. UCS gives this opportunity to 10th–12th graders who like to earn college credits. It helps since it lowers the number of college classes you would take, depending on your career.

Now, there are negative aspects of being in high school. The main problem is that despite the interracial community, some things feel like there's racism in the school. One example would be sports. When I was playing volleyball during 8th grade, I was one of the only players that never played. Even if I tried to put a lot of effort into receiving my playtime, it wasn't enough for my coach. I honestly gave up volleyball after that. It was unfair to play the same six players every time and rely only on them for the entire game. But guess what? The new coach did the same thing with my friend. What's the point of being on a team if you're on the bench the entire time? I don't want to assume anything, but I think they're prejudiced, if not a tiny bit. There are more negative aspects, but this problem is the main one in my opinion.

II

Our Lives

HOLIDAYS & TRADITIONS

Emily Walker

My favorite Halloween night happened in 2017.

For Halloween that year, I dressed up as Darth Vader, who was my favorite villain at the time. It was a polyester body suit with Darth Vader's armor printed on it in color and a plastic helmet I borrowed from my dad. It fastened in the back with velcro and I remember it being very thin. It had a cape as well, solid black and kind of fuzzy. I was so excited about what the night had in store for me and my family.

First, we went to our church's Halloween service, which also featured a small fall "festival". During the service, our pastor preached to us about the importance of loving one another and being generous in times of celebration. It didn't really stand out to my 11-year-old brain because I was too busy thinking about how funny it was that the pastor was dressed as bald Dracula. After the service, the festivities began. There was a mock "trick or treating", a "fish for candy", a costume contest, a cake walk, and a hay ride. I played all the games at least three times and then rode on the hay ride, of which I almost fell off. My family and I were there for almost three hours before we moved on to actually trick or treating.

We must have gone to at least 25 or 35 houses, collecting candy, pastries, and other treats while my baby sisters started crying because their tummies ached and their feet hurt. My parents rolled their eyes picked the two littlest ones up and carried them the rest of the way back to the car. They, in fact, just needed a short nap, which they took on the 45-minute drive to a classmate's house party that Sarah and I were invited to, and we anxiously agreed to since it was the first party we were ever invited to in at least 4 years.

As it turns out, we were the only children in 5th grade to show up, actually, we were the only kids other than the initial classmate to show up. Yet that was okay because there was plenty of food, candy, and drinks for only 6 children, it seemed as if they were prepared for a small army of starved children, not the meager handful of straggly kids that did. There was a banquet of cakes, meats, pasta, sugared candy fruits, and mounds of chocolates and hard candies. Honestly, I thought I would pass out from being so full and tired from everything I'd done that night.

We had to go home after an hour and some odd minutes. My classmate's mother wouldn't let us leave without giving each of us a plate of food for the following day and without filling our candy buckets to the brim. I was filled with a sleepy buzz of happiness and contentment as my dad had to round my family up and do head counts before driving away into the street lamp-lit night. I passed out on the way home and my dad probably carried me to bed. I came to this conclusion because I awoke in my bed and was very confused as to when exactly I got there.

In all, I had a wonderful time.

Clint McDonald

My favorite holiday is Christmas. I love drinking eggnog and listening to Christmas music. We buy the eggnog, but I would like to take the time to learn how to make it. One of my favorite presents was a PlayStation 5. Red Date REdemtion 2 is my favorite game. It is a cowboy game. Spending time with my family makes this holiday memorable each year. Sometimes, we go to the mall to shop. We have a family dinner at home because my mom doesn't like going to other people's homes.

My least favorite holiday is Halloween. My parents are very religious, and they consider it a devil's holiday. I've never been able to celebrate this holiday. I feel like I have missed out on it. We still buy candy, but I've only been trick-or-treating 1 time when I snuck out of the house as a 10-year-old. Old. My parents were really mad. They called the police because I was missing for 2 hours. I couldn't go outside to play for several months. I like being outside, so it was hard for me.

Kayla Harris

The charm of Christmas traditions brought warmth and happiness into my childhood home. A vibrant atmosphere was created by the traditional lights, the smell of freshly baked ham, and the excitement of opening gifts. However, our home's dynamics changed when I was a teenager. Maybe it was my dad's tragic death. At first, I believed this, but I'm not sure because we did have a few enjoyable Christmases following that. Considering how it seemed like everyone we knew, even some of our favorite relatives, simply drifted apart following my dad's death, perhaps it was the changes in family structure. There was such a void left by it...The excitement had given way to a sense of monotony, and I found myself missing the festive atmosphere that had defined our previous holiday gatherings.

If I could change something about our family's Christmas traditions, I would strive to recapture the nostalgic wreath that made the season so special during my childhood and hang it up on the front door. A new activity or the reintroduction of a tiny but important tradition could rekindle the sense of celebration that has faded over time. It might be possible to create a more inclusive and joyful experience for all family members by using components that represent their individual interests and personalities. It may be possible to close the gap between what makes of the past and the realities of the present by accepting change but keeping the core of cherished traditions.

The joy of spending time with one another and the celebration of love are ultimately what makes Christmas so special. Adapting our traditions to our family's changing dynamics guarantees that everyone, regardless of age or situation, will continue to feel the spirit of the holidays and enjoy them. Through cultivating an environment of coziness and empathy, and exchanging happiness, we can make enduring memories that last forever.

Anonymous

The thing I would like to change about my family traditions is that I'd start having ones based on family now, not what one individual wants. It seems so silly to say, but my family's traditions during the holidays are dictated by the past. I don't think my parents even realize that it controls and lingers over the holidays, I think they genuinely believe everyone wants to do the activities we used to, even if we've grown out of them and have done them forever and a day.

Most of our traditions include driving around to see lights other people put up, watching Christmas films from when my parents were 5 to 7 years old, and watching a Santa Tracker tell us where Santa is before bed, things from when we all were young. I understand what traditions are and that this could be yours as well, but all my siblings don't believe in Santa and the movies don't interest us because of our age and generation, the lights are the same every year and one of my siblings complain about the long drive and another about a headache.

The thing about traditions is that they evolve, they change, and everyone has an influence on what they are. I guess, I really just want something new to go with the old, or to have new interests in mind when planning. Not things from when we were young, but things we could do now. I want our traditions to grow with us, or to look into the future just a bit, that way I can have a tradition that I am not bored of for the future partner and kids I may have 10 years from now. I want to have a nostalgic starting point for my future traditions, not a repeat because I don't know what else to do.

Tavares Foster

I wouldn't change anything about my family traditions. I wouldn't change my family traditions because they are unique and special to my family and we have been doing them for years. They are also quite fun and we bond over them with each other quite well. One of our traditions is to bake some brownies with marshmallow fluff on top on special occasions. It's my favorite type of brownie and one of my favorite traditions to do with my family.

Another one of my favorite traditions is playing board games on Christmas day. One of my favorite board games is Monopoly, although it takes a long to play. My favorite thing about Monopoly is when I buy an expensive property and someone lands on it. Another one of my favorite board games is Sorry because it's all about sabotaging the other players. My favorite thing about Sorry is the bubble with the dice in the middle of the board because of the sound it makes. I usually get lucky and get double sixes.

Despite my family not having many traditions, we still have a lot of fun doing them. We have been doing these traditions for a long time and love doing them. I believe everyone should have at least one family tradition due to how fun they are. More importantly, people should do them to bond with their family more. Overall, traditions are important for having a good time with your family and bonding with them.

MY PLACE

Emily Walker

The pond down the road from my house is my favorite place because of the memories I have there, mainly of fishing and camping with my family members. The sound of the fish popping out of the water and the noises of the forest surrounding it are almost therapeutic. I go there with my family in the summer and camp in the winter. We have fun and I can really see how much fun my parents are also having. It's so close to my home that I could walk, pole, bait, and bucket in hand down to it and I could be fishing not even half a mile from my house.

It's your standard pond. It smells like plants and vegetation and all those icky smells you associate with ponds, it is at least 13 feet at its deepest and 2 feet in the shallows. The water is murky most days but on rare occasions, it is a clear tea-tinted pool that is teaming with life, fish, bugs, turtles, snakes, and even some beavers There is one sturdy structure, an old grey cabin, used for storage. It had been a fishing cabin of I-don't-even-know-how-many years previous. I heard it was blue at one point from my grandpa, who was probably a little boy when it was built. There is a rotting peer leading into the water where rusting, rotting boats are slowly disappearing from wear and weather.

This isn't to say it is less beautiful than other ponds, rather it holds a different kind of beauty. The squishy, smelly beauty of being the home to so many water dwellers for so many years and having the resulting muck settle into a slimy cradle for the water. The itchy beauty of forgetting your bug spray and fly swatter at home and subsequently being eaten by bugs. The summer's beauty of fishing on sunny days with coolers full of water, sodas, and melty popsicles for thirsty, hot, sunburnt kids who "Just don't see why this place is such a big deal." The painful learner's beauty of a hook snagging your skin, the smack of a pole whose line got stuck in the trees or debris in the water, and the cuts from being too clumsy with a knife. It holds that remembering kind of beauty from being told stories from your father's childhood, from your aunt's childhood, and your grandfather's childhood that you just can't seem to remember after you leave and cannot seem to ask about until you're back.

It's a real Southern type of place, with its own strange charm, and it's my home away from home. It isn't impressive and it doesn't need to be. That's the beauty of a humble pond in the blackbelt. To others, it might be a hole in the ground that holds water and critters, but to me, it might as well be my own little fountain of youth, a source of the kind of energy that I had when I was young, and a place full of memories I will never quite remember yet never quite forget. And all this is why it is my favorite place.

Avery Long

A community is a group of people living together within a larger society with a common characteristic or interest. Communities bring together people and allow them to get to know each other more. Different communities have many different places that allow people to come together. My place is Tres Hermanos in Livingston, Al.

Many people don't know where Mexican food comes from. The history of Mexican food can be traced back two thousand years. Both the Mayans and Aztecs influenced these methods of cooking and the dishes that are still seen today. Many towns have Mexican restaurants, but we only have one.

This is my favorite place around Sumter County because Mexican is my favorite food. This place is unique because it is the only restaurant near my house, which is 15 minutes away. I live in York, which has no good restaurants in town. We are lucky enough to have one restaurant that isn't even that good and is only open for 3-4 days a week.

Mexico has many delicious authentic Mexican dishes. Of course, I mainly go for the chips and dip. I also get different food every time I go. A few favorites are the Shrimp Fajitas, Shrimp Quesadillas, Taco Salads, Shrimp over Rice, and more. As you can see, I really like seafood, so luckily, I can just go to Mexico up the road and get shrimp with Mexican food. Two of my favorites!

Mexico means a lot to me. It is a place where I can reconnect with my family after a hard week. If my boyfriend and I go on dates, it's usually to Mexico because it is very convenient and delicious. We usually gossip and eat chips and dip. I have gone and eaten at Tres Hermanos ever since I was little. It gives me nostalgia every time I go, and it means a lot.

Aliyah Martin

Bonita Lakes is one of my favorite places because it's a great place to get outdoors. It's peaceful and lightly developed for paddling, fishing, hiking, and exercising. You can even bring your dog or horse! It has over 20 miles of equestrian trails wind through the trees and along the lake. This place is unique to me because I love the equestrian trails! Bonita Lakes equestrian trails consist of over 10 miles of flat land and hills along a lake shore. They have ample parking for horse trailers, wash space, and water for your horse!

Bonita Lakes is a friendly, peaceful getaway from indoors. A place where you could run, go fishing, ride your horse, or walk your dog. It is a great place! The city limits encompass the 3,300-acre Bonita Lakes Park. There are some downcasts of this place. If I could change anything about Bonita Lakes, it would be the owners of the dogs cleaning up behind their pets. I think it's unsanitary and disrespectful to the others who come out to enjoy Bonita Lakes.

The connection I feel to Bonita Lakes is all the great memories I've created there. I've been going to Bonita Lakes every Sunday with my family. This Sunday, we went with friends and walked around the lake. Walking around the lake when the sun sets is so pretty and peaceful. It reminds me of when I first visited Bonita Lakes in June 2021 with my aunt and a few cousins. We all walked around the lake one Sunday after church. It was very hot and I disliked it at first, but eventually, we went back, but this time, we fed the ducks! It was so much fun.

Hannah Prince

My favorite place is the lake in Livingston by the UWA gym. Why is it my favorite place? It is because it's very peaceful to see a lot of pretty birds and turtles, and there isn't much noise. Also, you can go fishing, go in the boa, or just sit and talk to the person you're with. You can find your first love, someone who's just like you, loves good vibes, doesn't bring bad vibes around, and also has a good personality. Also, you can walk around the lake to clear your mind if you have a lot going on and want to distance yourself from people.

What makes this place special is that there's no littering. Also, it's very quiet. All you can hear is the birds chirping. And there's a trail you can go on while you are there. You can probably ride your four-by-four back there or you can walk with the person you are with. You can just enjoy the nature while you're walking and talking. The last thing that makes this place special is that you can take your family there and have a nice family time, bring your friends, or just you or your love interest.

The lake is very peaceful with no loud noises and pretty birds. There are no bad smells or signs of paved streets or traffic. Ducks and turtles surround the lake. You can bring a little snack while you are there because there are picnic tables for you to sit at if you get tired of walking in and want to take a little break to enjoy the sounds of nature.

The first time I went there was probably in 2019 or 2020. I went with my science teacher. It was fun, and I enjoyed walking to get there. It was worth the walk. My favorite part was the trail. It was a lot of walking, but I didn't mind. We crossed over a little bridge, and I saw a turtle. It was so cute and tiny. It was a walking field trip. I have not been there in a while. I hope it is still the same as it was back then.

I would not change anything about this place because it's so peaceful there. It helps clear your mind if you have a very long day. Also, it could bring your family close together because there's not that many people to distract you. There are pretty birds in the water, and it's just so breathtaking. I hope it's as perfect as I imagined.

Traeger Stephens

My favorite place is a pasture and the pond at my grandad's place in Coatopa outside of Livingston. I like seeing the cows and seeing the bass and the bream jump out of the water. I caught one of my best bass fish there, which was 6.12 oz. My favorite thing to do there is to ride my four-wheeler around the pasture and down the dirt road. When family friends are over, I usually let the younger kids ride on my four-wheeler. It's one of the first things they want to do when they arrive. The dirt road is mostly dusty-red, but it can sometimes be rough and muddy from people mud-riding in their trucks.

Recently, we had a dove shoot. One of the younger boys wanted to ride with me instead of sitting in the dusty dove field. After riding, he sat in the field with us behind a hay bale. He didn't like the loud *pop*s of gunfire.

I enjoy feeding the cows with my dad. We feed them pellets and hay. Sometimes it's so muddy in the cow pasture the truck will slide into the cow troughs. Cows love to hit and bump into the truck when we're out there. This truck looks rough! It's never been cleaned, and it's seen better days.

Anonymous

My favorite place would be Jaycee Park in Livingston, AL. I am 100 percent a homebody, and going out is something that is not on my to-do list, unlike my sisters. However, if I am caught on the right day, a day or even an evening in the park would do my mind some good.

Jaycee Park is unique to me because I feel like it is actually a place where I can talk the most to others. When I am at home, I tend to keep to myself and not talk that much. Pretty much, I stay in my own little bubble. Going to the park kind of encourages me to open up a bit.

To describe Jaycee Park, I would say it is a place in my small town where people can get together and enjoy their time, whether it is in the morning time, when it is relatively quiet and peaceful, or in the evening when it is more lively and populated. Parties and games are often held there as Jaycee Park seems like a go-to for many.

Some of my favorite memories of going to Jaycee Park consist of going with some of my cousins a few years ago. They stay in Tuscaloosa, so I don't get to see them as much as I want to since they moved there. So, on occasion, whenever they would visit me and my family, we would all decide to go to the park. I'm not sure what it was, but getting on my usual swing on the right side, and having my younger sister and cousin on theirs just incited our own little catch-up sessions. We would talk about things we missed, or sort of gossip and share some secrets. I mean, we could talk until it got dark outside. That's just how engrossed we were in the conversations. I'm not exactly sure when I visited Jaycee Park for the very first time, but I'm pretty sure my cousins were a part of it.

As much as I hate to say it, I'd have to change the swing set. It has held its own for many years and has many memories, but it is time to say goodbye. I feel like a new swing set would bring more color and life back into the park.

LEARNING EXPERIENCE

Lennon Phillips

The biggest learning point in my life was my dad and the issues he struggles with. I learned from a very young age that even your family will let you down, and sadly, I learned this the hard way. My dad has struggled with drug use my entire life. I rarely saw him when I was younger because he was in and out of rehab. Of course, I didn't know this when I was younger. All I knew was that my father wanted little to nothing to do with me. It is very hard to say that it was not completely his fault, but in the back of my mind, I will always have a slight discomfort with the man and what he has done to me. Although he tries to fix it I can not fully accept the fact that he had nothing to do with my younger self.

Even though he has done all of these things, and many people do not find anything positive, I do. I have learned to be careful with my actions and who I associate myself with. I have learned that everyone, including myself, has to work hard mentally and physically to have good things in life.

Amarion Dubose

An event that I have learned from is when I'm in a bad situation, I can always call anyone for help. In the past, I was in a lot of situations that all of a sudden came out of the blue, and the next step I thought was how to avoid, or even attempt to fix it. The decision I have chosen was to fix it, but now as a teenager, I have learned asking for help is the only solution when being in a situation that can be scary, overwhelming, or horrid. It took a while for me to realize that there was nothing wrong with going to an adult and telling them about what happened. A week ago, I was in a bad situation that didn't have anything to do with me, and when I heard about it, It caught me off guard because I didn't have any idea of what was going on, or how my name was brought up from the start. After I heard the news, I ran to the restroom in distress, calling my dad crying to check me out of school due to the fact another rumor had been going around without me realizing it at the last minute.

Out of fear, I stayed hidden in the restroom until my mom arrived to check me out and to avoid going into the lunchroom where everybody else was. Before I left, my mom wanted the counselors to find out what had happened, because my dad had called my mom and told her about what I told him when I called him 10 minutes earlier. Afterward, I told both my mom and the counselors my side of the story because I wanted mine to be heard, and that I didn't have any involvement in what everyone had been saying or what had been done.

I've tried to run away from the issue because when a rumor says something that's not true, it spreads absolutely quickly from one person to another. Nowadays, everyone will believe what they hear first without knowing the actual truth. I learned that you can't always run from a problem, and that the best thing to do is face it.

Matthew Kendrick

It would be difficult to name precisely the most profound learning experience in my life. But, one of my most profound learning experiences was when I first communicated in French with a native speaker. I am not quite sure what we even talked about; I don't even know his name. It was just important that we did speak. Also, it was not actual verbal communication, only texting. But still, it counts as my first encounter with a native speaker.

I was playing video games when I saw a Quebecer in my game, so I messaged him on the platform in French. Again, I do not know what we talked about, but I made it clear that I was still a learner. He showed his grace to me, and more importantly, he educated me and pointed out my mistakes. Our monthly character trait of February is kindness. He could have just told me that my grammar was perfect, but instead he extended his kindness to me and told me what I did wrong. He taught me some slang and abbreviations that a textbook or YouTube video would never think to teach.

I will never forget my brief experience with that kind stranger, or the intense vertigo I felt. Thanks to him, I have improved greatly since then. One of my greatest accomplishments that might not mean anything to anyone else, is when I commented on a music video by one of my favorite French singers. That comment received hundreds of likes and several replies that corrected a few minor grammatical errors, which goes to show that the learning process never ends. I believe that that may never have happened without that first learning experience.

Zy'Kirea Long

I would not call it a learning experience more like a lesson taught. It was Thanksgiving weekend and my family came down including my auntie Na'Kida. Everyone was out getting things for dinner and my Auntie Kida, my cousin Nariya, the twins, and I went to Meridian to get some things so I could show them around. When we got to Walmart, it was time for one of the twins' dippers to be changed and they were at an age where they move a lot and twists and turns a lot. So later that day we got back to my grandma's house where everyone was staying and I let the twins down to play. There was a gas heater in the kitchen where everyone was sitting and one of the twins was about to pull up on it. My auntie Kida was calling me to come get him, but I wasn't going to get to him on time and he was about to touch the heater. Kida went to see if the heater was hot, but she only touched one part of the heater, not the red part where it would be hot. Shireeya and I both went into the kitchen to get him. My auntie Kida was talking to me and me, being so smart-mouthed I said, *gurl, you can't even change a dipper* (she was about to put it on backward). She heard me and called me to come here but I knew she was mad so I did not turn around to her. When she came and pulled me to the side, she was asking me what was wrong with me and why did I not answer her when she called. I just stood there with an attitude, but when she told me she was going to remove herself from grown kids and she wasn't going to say anything else to me, I really did not care because, to this day, no one knows why I have such a bad attitude but me.

Hannah Price

One event was when it was a church event and I volunteered to speak in front of the whole church because no one else wanted to do the speaking part. It was a scary experience. I really didn't have the confidence to speak in front of them. I started to stutter, then I spoke so low that people couldn't hear me and it sounded like I was about to cry. However, I learned from this experience to keep practicing and have confidence in myself to speak in front of people, take deep breaths before I start reading, take my time, and speak a little louder so they can understand what I'm saying. I would like to say I'm not the only person who gets nervous when speaking in front of a crowd of people, but I would like just to tell them we have to believe that we can do it. I wouldn't stop speaking in front of people just have faith that you can do it.

Another event was Praise dancing. When the twins asked me to do a praise dance with them, I told them yeah even if I was scared. I still said yes because I hadn't Praise dance in a while so we went together. I messed up a couple of times. I was getting irritated because they had not and I felt like I was holding them up because we had more parts to practice. But what I did was I went home and started to practice until I got it. It took me minutes but I got it, so the next time we practiced, I got the hang of it. On the day of the event when we had to dance, I was really nervous because, like I said, I hadn't practiced in a while, so

I was super nervous but it turned out okay. We did really well. We did mess up a little bit, but we kept going with our dance. I would say for the event never give up keep practicing until you get it because if you give up too quickly, that will not get you anywhere at all.

Zamiyah Rice

Arriving at this school as a new student was the most profound learning experience. Seeing so many different people made me nervous. It was a culture shock, and I felt out of place. I thought It would be impossible for me to "fit in". Making friends was never easy for me to do. But after some time adjusting to my new environment, I found a group of people who were just as weird as me. I learned that whatever I go and no matter the circumstances, the people I'll bond with will eventually come.

Addyson Tillman

The most profound learning experience was meeting a girl in the seventh grade. I was so infatuated with the idea that she would like me; meeting this girl was like a breath of fresh air in making a new friend since I never really had good friends at my old school.

Trying to make friends at my old school was the hardest thing for me. Teachers would make us do these pairing-up projects and nobody ever wanted to be with me. Until now, I did not know why. All I did was exist in the school, and I was shunned in it. It was bad. I ended up going to the counselor, but she did not help in the comfort department. So, I told my parents about it, and they did nothing. Why? At the time, my brother was a junior when we talked, so they wanted to let him finish his time in high school there. Which, I was so opposed to the idea. Finally, he graduated, though.

Me and that girl were inseparable; nobody could do anything to get us apart. If my phone was taken away, that would be fine. I had a console. This led to us getting very close to one another. Like, we were catching feelings close. She was giving me something I did not get often – attention. When we talked, I felt like I was being listened to. I loved that. I loved the attention. In three classes, I would slip my phone out just to text her… and not so discreetly. My teachers did not do anything about it, so of course I took it as a green light to keep going. Why? Because I had the ache to continue to talk to her all day, every day. We'd stay up together and sleep on the phone. My parents hated that we would sleep on call. I never figured out why. Eventually, we became so close that we met. Meeting her was so good. Maybe there is not a word to explain how I felt we met. Ecstasy is not enough of a word. I remember just going into her arms for the first time and melting when I touched her. We even shared our food when we ate out, that is how close we were. We did everything together. And I am not exaggerating when I say that we did everything together.

We had to separate, though. And I mean permanently, after all of that. It hurt so bad. School got hard after we separated, not like it was not hard before, but it got worse. Even in all of this, I was able to see and not overlook what I had come to realize. If not then, she would go eventually, so there was no point in me trying to keep someone that had come to replace me. That is not the friendship I needed. And I learned that letting go of people that would just hurt you, in the long run, was the best decision. The ache to talk to her was still there, but I stayed off my phone… Mostly.

Angel Burrell

A lesson that I have learned over the years is not to take anything for granted. Life is too short to still hold grudges towards others. You have to live and let go. Give your problems to God, and let him help you solve them. In some situations, you're not going to get the answer you are looking for, but he is trying to better you. God sees farther than us, and he knows what is going to help prevent us and what's not going to prevent us from meeting our potential. This has changed my outlook on different people in life and situations.

Emily Walker

A lesson I learned recently is one I never really thought about until I was lying in bed last night feeling lonely for a person I haven't talked to in forever. The lesson was that nostalgia lies to you or doesn't tell you the whole truth about the thing you were thinking so wistfully about.

Nostalgia is the feeling you have when you see Lofthouse cookies in Walmart and remember all those schoolhouse Christmas parties from when you were in elementary school. Those cookies were so yummy back then, so you find yourself buying them and taking them home to enjoy. But when you open the package and taste the cookie, you remember they never tasted good. You remember them tasting good because you were having fun and nostalgia makes you forget that weird powder taste. Nostalgia takes that feeling you had, that happiness and excitement, and ties everything nicely in a bowed present for you to cherish.

Nostalgia makes you forget that your heart ached and wept for hours when you were with that person, but you just remember those special, rare occasions when they showed that they loved you and you want to go back to that love. Nostalgia makes you forget that you didn't really take an interest in what that friend was saying, you just remember that they were really happy talking to you. And nostalgia makes you forget what exactly made your cousin have no contact with your family, you just miss her even if she hasn't been there for you in years and you want to play like you used to when you were kids.

Nostalgia makes you miss those things and makes you wonder why you ever stopped doing that activity you really liked, or why you haven't kept up with that TV show you watched a couple of months ago, and it makes you ponder why you haven't talked to that person you swore you couldn't live without just a year ago. But there's a reason for all of it. You stopped knitting because it took up too much time from your priorities, that show fired all of your favorite cast members, and that person that you needed wasn't there for you so many times you might as well have been alone. Nostalgia is the greatest feeling, but it is also the greatest illusion of a better past.

The lesson is that you cannot live in the present with those foggy rose-tinted glasses, nostalgia blinds you to the present and divides your reasoning. Be careful when you feel this way, there's a reason everything happened the way it did.

WHEN DID YOU LAST...

Shaquon Lee

...Show Gratitude?

The last time I showed gratitude to someone was last week. It was my grandma. I started to clean the house when she asked me to because I could never say no to my grandma. She gets me anything I ask for. Not only that, sometimes I can spend the day without even cleaning up because she does it most of the time. But yes, I showed gratitude by cleaning the house. I also sometimes clean out her car before she goes somewhere. I tend to cut the grass when it looks a little off or bad. Cleaning is the way I show my grandma gratitude.

Another way I show my grandma gratitude is by using manners or cooking when she doesn't feel like it. I also wash dishes after my family eats every night. I feel like my grandma deserves all the gratitude in the world, especially for raising me.

Ana S. Montaño Alanis

...Show Gratitude?

The last time I showed gratitude to someone was about 15 minutes ago when my friend passed me one of my bags while I was packing my things and getting ready to leave class. It seems a bit underwhelming, and I was hesitant to put this example precisely because I found it anticlimactic. In the end, I decided to include it, partly because, one, the example wouldn't be true, and two, the example was completely valid. Absolutely valid, even though it doesn't feel like it.

When showing gratitude, or at least, when you write about an example when you were showing gratitude, your mind automatically tries to jump to what might be considered more "important" or "impactful." To an example where you swelled with pride after showing gratitude.

However, I don't think that I particularly feel anything major, really, after saying thanks to someone. Instead, I feel something *before* saying thanks to someone: a combination of gratitude and obligation, the latter drilled into me by my relatives as a small kid so I could grow up with basic decency. I think it's that, honestly, I mean, that invokes a thank you from someone and not a thank you that invokes gratefulness or internal fulfillment.

I'm not sure if that is a common, naturally occurring thing. That is, feeling internal fulfillment. I have never really thought to myself after expressing gratitude, *Man, I feel so happy to have said thank you.* I guess it's because I express gratitude regularly in small tidbits and passing thanks, so they don't really stand out as "special enough" to feel fulfilled.

However, sometimes I do feel happy and glad to have said thank you, not because of the words I said but because of the repercussions: a tiny smile, a happy "You're welcome." *That* makes me happy if I'm paying enough attention to notice. I'm happy when others are glad they're appreciated.

Ana S. Montaño Alanis

...Have Fun?

I can remember that, during summer vacation, I had a smile permanently fixed on my face. Seeing people I don't usually see made me unmeasurably happy. I can say with confidence that I had fun.

But, that probably wasn't the most recent time I had fun.

When I came back to the U.S. and spent my days lazying at home, I remember having movie marathons with my sisters and playing anything from board games to electronic ones. We had cookouts and watched movies in theaters. I am positively sure that I had fun during those times.

But, was that really the most recent time I had fun?

I've thought that I haven't had fun in school—actually, I thought that just yesterday—but that probably isn't true. I probably had fun during it, in some mundane fragment of my time surrounded by other mundane fragments of my time. Maybe the only reason I remember it as mundane was because it was surrounded by those other mundane times, or maybe because of the normality of having slight fun in school. It's normal, so it becomes less special, being overshadowed by a greater happiness that came before or after.

It wasn't until now, until I really reflect on it, that I came to realize that I do have fun. I do smile and joke in class with my friends, regardless of the workload. It's just, at the end of the day, when you start thinking of homework and practice and other time-consuming activities that you still have to do, those moments end up on the back burner. Forgotten.

I think the last time I had fun was today. I was joking around with one of my friends in History and, during lunch, I sat with some other friends and talked about things that probably had no relation to each other but somehow made sense conversation-wise. I played a matching game with the kid I was tutoring, and we both really got into it, seeing how fast we could complete it in different variations. I had fun today.

I had fun today.

Imagine *that*. I didn't really realize it until now. Funny thing, isn't it?

TEENS

Sadie Carter

The hardest part about being a teenager is finding purpose and identity. As a Christian, I know my identity is in Jesus, but even for me, I struggle to know who I am and what my purpose is. Being a teenager is highly confusing. There are so many things going on at once, and everyone is handling them differently. According to APA, over 20% of teens have seriously considered suicide. Being a teenager myself, I know people who have struggled with these thoughts, and unfortunately, I have lost people to these thoughts. Finally, being a teenager is hard because when it comes down to it, we feel alone, we feel like no one understands us, and we feel as if no one would really miss us if we simply disappeared.

Justin Clarke

The hardest thing about being a teenager is finding a balance between being a kid and an adult. Teenagers have to take on the responsibility of taking care and providing for themselves. We have to start getting a job to pay for our own things and do other things our parents would usually do for us. But since we aren't adults, we still want to go out and have fun. There are things that we could do ourselves, but instead, we want our parents to do it for us. This is what I believe is the hardest thing about being a teenager.

A.J.

My business shows the characteristics of a teenager having creativity. "CookiesbyMarii" shows creativity in many ways. Those ways that I think about in my business are exploratory, designing skills, and the basic skills of creativity.

CookiesbyMarii shows several ways I explore being creative. For example, I explore new ingredients, new ways to decorate, ways to promote my cookies, etc. I use many different ingredients which help me come up with the flavors I have on my menu. It is not an easy process, but with the encouraging words from my mother and having God by my side, with anything that I do, I know that my business will soon become successful. It's not the biggest business, but I can see it going far one day.

My designing skills come in when it's time to decorate my cookies. While decorating, I focus and really use my ability to think. It's a certain way that I design my cookies. Although I've been running my business for a while, I still tend to mess up, which is alright. Over time, my mistakes only helped me get better at what I do. I consider this as a learning process because every time I mess up, I learn from my mistakes and keep learning and progressing.

Presentation, in my opinion, is a needed skill if you are in a business. You need to know how to present your product to get sales. For me, my product is my cookies. Not only do they look nice but they taste delicious, so I feel like that's a great thing when it comes to my business. Presentation is the key to getting sales and recognition.

Being the CEO of a business is not an easy job. You need to have skills such as great communication, being respectful, being able to listen, etc. However, you can be anything you want to be in life. If you put your mind to it and continue being passionate about it, you will succeed with anything.

MUSIC & ART

Angel Burrell

The song "Sorrows" by Bryson Tiller revolves around the feelings of loneliness and abandonment the protagonist experiences after a break-up. He feels that his ex-girlfriend, who used to be his close friend, has changed and left him behind. The lyrics in the first verse suggest that the protagonist is struggling to come to terms with the end of the relationship and the disappointment he feels in his once-close friend. He is left questioning everything that his ex-girlfriend had told him about her feelings towards him.

In the chorus, the protagonist expresses his willingness to be there for his ex-girlfriend if she needs him. He tells her that he will always be available if she ever wants or needs his company. This highlights the fact that the protagonist still has feelings for his ex-girlfriend and is hoping to renew their relationship.

The post-chorus hints at the fact that the protagonist is aware that he and his ex-girlfriend are no longer on the same page and that their friendship is not as close as it used to be. He is in pain and is struggling to come to terms with the end of their relationship.

The second verse shows the protagonist exploring the idea of moving on from his ex-girlfriend and possibly seeing someone else. However, he repeatedly hints that he is not ready to start afresh without his ex-girlfriend and is struggling to come to terms with his emotions.

The song "Sorrows" will always be my favorite song to listen to. I loved the way Bryson expressed his feelings in the lyrics. He made the listeners feel every line and verse he sang in the song. The song tells about the pain of his heartbreak and how he is trying to get over his ex-girlfriend daily. He is looking for closure but he still has plenty of love for her throughout the song as he explains the lyrics. I love this song because it speaks to the regret of not stopping the decline of our environment, and describes the resulting wasteland.

Tavares Foster

Ivan the Terrible and His Son

By: Ilya Repin

Ivan the Terrible and His Son is a piece by Russian artist Ilya Repin between 1883 and 1885. It depicts a horrified and grief-ridden Ivan the Terrible holding his dying son. It is implied or assumed that Ivan struck his son in the head in a fit of rage but most likely immediately regretted it. The fear and despair in Ivan's eyes are masterfully shown as he's cradling his son. The single tear on his son's face shows his sorrow in his dying moments.

Repin began the painting in Moscow, starting off with a sketch in 1882. Repin had multiple inspirations for the painting. The main inspiration was the violence and revenge from the political events of 1881. Another inspiration was Nikolai Rimsky-Korsakov's music. Lastly, the bullfights he witnessed in Western Europe.

This painting is one of my favorites because it shows how much emotion art can depict and evoke in someone. I also appreciate the time dedicated to making the painting, as it took 4 years to finish it. I believe it is one of the best paintings from the 1800s and is a masterpiece. The painting is probably one of the best depictions of grief and regret. It is truly a work of art and is one of my favorites.

Kayla Harris

The song I chose is "Dark Red" by Steve Lacy. I'm not sure how to describe it, the feeling I mean. My mind kind of just shifts when I listen to music, but specifically, the ones by Steve Lacy put me in my own little universe, one where I imagine scenarios with my own characters and stories that fit the song. With "Dark Red", I can come up with so many different stories, whether it be with my characters or just myself. It's like little movies or something. Like I said, it is hard to explain.

After some research, I found something called maladaptive daydreaming, which I think I may suffer from. It's where you basically daydream more than usual and even have your own characters and plots that take place. Inevitably, you're separating yourself from the real world to imagine a better one or one that is more enjoyable at the time. It can be really damaging in the long run because you could eventually separate yourself from reality so much that you don't really focus on what's right in front of you or nothing is as good as you want it to be.

For me, I always start my playlists off by listening to "Dark Red", and when I do, in my mind it's like becoming the camera in a movie. I immediately see a group of friends, specifically six. Three girls, three boys with myself being one of the girls. I can not tell you why, but this group of friends basically have at least 4 hours' worth of movie plots. And it's been like this since 2020, which I think gave me time to just think more about what I want in life. I know this because I can remember the first time I thought about it. But anyway, listening to Steve Lacy's music just kinda brings it to life, and you know, it's not just this song. "Show My How" by Men I Trust, "Chambers of Reflection" by Mac DeMarco, "Little Dark Age" by MGMT, and "Cigarettes Out The Window" by TV Girl are just some of the stars that shine around my universe.

In a way, I feel like they are the type of group of friends that I want, the type of relationship I imagine with someone. Sometimes I think I set my standards so high for things like this because just being around the people that surround me, specifically at school where you think you'd meet your future lifelong friends or significant other, I immediately get disappointed by the type of people they are and get pulled back down from my universe of bliss to reality. And what sucks more is thinking in the beginning you finally find at least one person that could possibly fit in your universe, only for the stars reflecting in their eyes to not be what they seem.

...You know, when I think about it now, even though he was older than me, he just really acted like his age too much, <u>young and dumb</u>. Ugh, that's what I get for being so mature for my age...

Emily Walker

How the song " 7 Years " by Lukas Graham makes me feel...

The song " 7 Years" is about how everything was so grand and simple when you were young, about how it feels to grow older, and the success or failure you can encounter during your life. I first remember hearing this song when I was around 8 and I didn't quite understand it or know how to feel about it. Now, almost 10 years later, I think I have a faint understanding of its message.

When we were young it seemed like the future was so far away, that we had all the time and friends in the world. Boys were icky, girls were silly, and friends were just people that happened to be in your life that you made instantly. When we were young I remember the job most girls wanted was "princess," and for the boys, it was "Monster Truck Driver". It seems to be a lifetime ago when I didn't have to worry about my plan for life or how I'd be going to college.

As I've grown older I have noticed that being an adult is so close. 30 feels like it's running up to catch me, friends are something I have to put effort into, people are more complicated, and the future is not as bright. It's rather scary. I find myself thinking about my future, what job am I going to have, who is going to be with me for the rest of my life, whether I will have kids, whether I will live to see 60, and if my parents will be around for another 40 years. I worry and wonder about what life I'll lead, whether or not it will be something I can look back on and smile at when I'm grey.

This song makes me wonder and think, it makes me emotional and solemn, and it makes me want to simultaneously visit the past or see into the future. I know time is ever-flowing and we are continuously marching forward into the future, but I cannot help but be excited and anxious. I wonder if I'll have a life that was worth the struggles.

Anonymous

Vulture Baby

"Home is ahead,
    Who needs the coast?
    Sometimes the gods
Just answer hope." - Blood Orange

As Spotify shuffled random songs on my TV, one particular song began playing. It sounded serene, like rain plummeting on the roof of a house. I let the song play, distracted by my tasks at the moment. Little did I know, that song would be the shoulder I leaned on whenever I sought solace.

I let the way I feel define me. It's a bad habit that I've had for a long time. I look at myself as something that needs to be "fixed" when that's far from the truth. I'm not a wound, I'm a person with a wound.

I often let other people influence me too easily. I fit in with the people around me like a puzzle piece. Who I am at school is different than me at home, online, or outside in a typical setting. Who I am is a blur to me. I've always been far from reach.

I try to do better and make a change in myself. It feels like a wall is blocking me from where I want to be and who I want to be. I know that to sail beyond the sunset, I must accept where I am in the present moment. It's easier said than done. To be ignorant is a blessing and to be aware is a curse. I know what needs to be changed, but how can I change it?

The song "Vulture Baby" reminds me of the color brown. It's an overwhelming source of comfort that I need in my life. It soothes me like a vulture soothing its baby. I interpret the lyrics as a message of hope. Sometimes, the only thing that keeps a person going is hope. Hope is the small ounce of light that shines in the darkest places.

I believe that all things come from within. The only thing that defines you is you. That fact brings me true peace. "Vulture Baby" reassures me of that. Everything that happens, happens. Hope is simple but it's strong.

Jaylon Amerson

NBAYoungBoy's music covers a range of emotions, from pain and hardship to success and resilience. His ability to convey raw emotions through his lyrics and delivery resonates with listeners who may find solace or connection in his music. He often addresses current trends, social issues, and growing up in certain environments while making his music culturally relevant to a significant audience.

Zy'Kirea Long

"Power" by The Clark Sisters

When the song starts, you're immediately hit with the sister's beautiful voice. The voices of each sister have a rich harmonious sound. This song is a masterpiece of all the gospel. The sisters have so much vocal power. They started singing at a very young age. Their voices were being trained by their mother, Dr. Mattie Moss Clark. To me, this song is a testament to the indomitable human spirit and it serves as a reminder of the power that lives within each one of us. This song has a different meaning for other people but what it means to me is a source of motivation and inspiration during difficult times in life. It reminds me that I have the power within myself to overcome obstacles and achieve goals. The lyrics that stood out to me were, *Sometimes I feel like I'm so all alone I felt so desperate and couldn't carry on The devil tried to shut me down and take away my crown I tried to leave, it captured me and tried to pull me down.* The Sisters came out with "the return album" during the pandemic.

Jamya James

When I listen to R&B music, it makes me feel like I'm traveling back to the 90s because of the vibe the music gives me. My favorite RNB song is Use Your Heart by -SWV. This song is one of my favorite 90s songs from back in the day. My mom and I get up almost every morning at 10 o'clock to clean up and listen to this song. Some R&B songs make me feel like I'm older than I am. I also like listening to blues my favorite song is We're Getting Careless With Our Love by -Johnnie Taylor. I like this song because it gives me the feeling that I'm living in the 80s. After all, that's the date Johnnie Taylor released the song. My mom was the first person to introduce me to blues she would sit in her room all day and listen to this specific song. Johnnie Taylor was known as the blues wailer he grew up in West Memphis performing gospel songs before he started working on creating blues songs. One of Johnnie Taylor's greatest hits is Soul Heaven. Johnnie released the hit song Soul Heaven in the year 1999.

Addyson Tillman

I have a favorite song, but it is not what most people think it might be. People always assume that I would listen to country music, pop, trap music, or anything of the sort. But, no. I like rock; alternative, metal, all of the genres that correlate to that kind of music. My favorite song is titled, "Lying is the Most Fun A Girl Can Have Without Taking Her Clothes Off."

This one-of-a-kind song is written by the famous "Panic! At the Disco" band. They were highly popular back when their first album. "A Fever You Can't Sweat Out", came out in 2004. This album is one of my favorite albums to exist. When I first heard of this song, it was April 2023, and I was resting on my bed. I had my Alexa playing the AFYCSO album, and this song played. I paused my game and asked my Alexa what the name of the song was. That was the starting point of my love for the genre of music. I did research and found out that the boys who sang and wrote the songs were 18 or 19. The singer was Brendon Urie, whilst the guitarist and songwriter was Ryan Ross. I like this whole album, except for the song "Nails For Breakfast, Tacks For Snacks." I just do not like the song's use of autotune. I was not born when the band had all four original members– some disbanded in 2009 before I was born. So no. I have never been to one of their concerts. My love for genres like this can not be overridden by any other, because I relate to the songs in those genres more than anything else. That is my story with my favorite song.

TRAVEL

Matthew Kendrick

If I could travel anywhere in the world, it would be to France. I would, of course, want to move around in the continent and explore other countries, but I would like to visit France first. The food and the culture entice me. More importantly, I would like to challenge myself to survive in a foreign land.

French food is an icon of delicacy across all Western cultures. The fanciest dishes that can be imagined probably include beef steak, perhaps even strange foods like escargot. In fact, escargot is just the French word for snail. I have always wanted to visit a French bakery in the early morning and buy a *pain au chocolat*, which literally means chocolate bread. All the good food seems like such an upgrade from dirty American microwaved food, which all Europeans vehemently hate.

It's a part of their culture to get fresh food always. They even keep their refrigerators just a little bit cooler than room temperature because they don't believe in storing food for as long as Americans do. The culture extends far beyond food; it includes the language and the music as well. I thoroughly enjoy the music that comes out of France, specifically from the city of Nantes (pronounced "n-aunt"). That is where I would go first, specifically.

I would go there all by myself in order to challenge myself. Learning a language means nothing if you can't actually use it in real life. If I took someone with me, I would depend on them like a crutch. I have to get rid of my crutches and get outside of my comfort zone to get the full experience and learn and grow as a person.

Of all the places in the world I could go, I would pick Nantes, France. I love the food and music that comes from that city, and I love learning about other cultures. I would also like to visit other places, like Italy, for all the same reasons. But, Nantes is at the very top of my list, and I know I will go there soon.

Amarion Dubose

If I could travel anywhere, it would be every city that has the most population in the United States. I would take my crew of friends with me because when we are together we laugh, joke, and goof off a lot, and it would be a great idea for them to come along. Bringing them on the journey would be epic, due to the fact we like clowning with each other. I can imagine my crew and I in either New York City or Los Angeles, especially with Va'dale with us because of his extreme sense of humor. It would be crazy in a hilarious way.

Since I'm into making shows and films, I can make a movie with us traveling around the USA. It would be like an adventure where everyone can see us traveling to the most popular cities, and as a comedy where we can show our wild and goofy side. Everyone might think I'm just a quiet guy but I do have goofy moments, especially when I'm with my friends. As I was writing this essay, I was thinking, what if this actually happened in real life? My crew and I are the class of 2024 and we can celebrate it by traveling all over the USA, that could be our epic event yet.

While on the adventure, I was thinking that we could find anything to do. I mentioned before that I can make a film of our adventure, we can go to an NBA game, go to a park and play football or just be silly. The best thing we probably can do is go to a trampoline park because that's a good place for us to be goofy with the cotton cube they have.

To be honest, we really don't have to go to far-away cities to have fun. It can be right here in the South.

The reason for saying that is because we were born and raised down here, that's all we are used to. We could go to Atlanta, Panama City, or even New Orleans. Three of us like to fish and hunt, and all together, we do like sports, such as basketball, football, and baseball. If we want to go to a beach somewhere, it can be Pensacola, Mobile, or Biloxi. If we did all this, that would be an adventure to remember for our senior year.

Going on an adventure to different places in the country with your friends is a wonderful idea to come up with. The fact that we are graduating from high school would be a great way to celebrate it, or even after graduation, we do it then. With my crew around, it's always a good time, and I can imagine what it would be like if we went on an adventure with the games we like to play, including our favorite one: running 15 or 30 seconds to see who will get tired first. It might sound ridiculous but in the end, it's serious, that's just us clowning. I do know that we can always hang with each other while we are still in school.

Zy'Kirea Long

If I could go anywhere in the world, it would be Napa, California. It is a beautiful place. The houses are massive out there. I love how the country part looks. The houses are far back, off the road. Napa is known for its hospitality, fine food, and luxury hotels. People go there for wind but I'll go for the fun of it. I'd take my sister Ja'Nyia and or my Auntie Kida only because of their fun. I'd have long, funny talks while on the road for 19 hours. One of my dreams is to move out there on my land and have a farm while working as a nurse.

Tamaya Tolliver

When I traveled to New Jersey during the summer, there were a lot of things that I discovered. Some things wouldn't shock you, but they surprised me while I was there. I'll be telling you about my trip to New Jersey.

The idea was my dad's, who wanted to visit my sister, Brianna, in Newark, New Jersey. We had planned a time to go up there sometime in late July. We could only stay a few days since DJ and I had to get ready for school to start soon. Once the time came, we drove to Nashville, Tennessee, and dropped the car off. Newark is a long way, so we went by airplane from Nashville. It was my second time riding an airplane and my dad and brother's first time. We had to wait for an hour before getting on our plane. Since most seats were taken, we sat on the ground beside each other and played on our phones. While we waited, Da dared DJ to sit by the window since it was his first time. DJ accepted the dare.

We had a lot of people going to Newark, so it was a while before we got on the plane. Once we settled down, we had to wait another thirty to forty-five minutes before the plane took off. It was because they were checking the weather or something else. Soon, the plane took off, and we were in the air for two hours. Da and DJ fell during the ride asleep, so I was the only one awake. I wasn't comfortable sleeping on an airplane yet.

After two hours, we landed in Newark. Now I thought it would be a little cold up there. I don't know why I was expecting it. To my surprise, it was SO hot. It is hotter than Alabama, and Alabama is HOT in the summer! We had to wait outside the airport about 10 minutes before Brianna's mother and grandmother came to pick us up. Then we headed to their apartment.

Once we got there, we saw Brianna waiting for us at the door. I immediately greeted and hugged her since it's been a long time since I saw her. She greeted us back and helped us get our luggage in the apartment. We talked for a bit before Da decided to take us to the store. We all hopped in the car and went to a store I never heard of before. It was the Newark version of Market Place. When we arrived, we grabbed food and drinks like cereal, Capri Suns, milk, cheese, etc. While the adults shopped, my siblings and I played around in the store. Joking, pushing each other, and just having a good time. We headed home once my dad bought everything.

After that, we chilled at the apartment while trying to find something to do. I had to do my work for my economics class, so I was busy during my trip. As we were thinking about what to do, someone suggested we get pizza and wings. Da ended up ordering it from Papa John's, and he, along with the other adult, went to go get it. That leaves me, Brianna, and DJ at the house by ourselves. Brianna and DJ hung out while I did my work. After about 15 minutes, the adults finally came back with our food. Boy, it was good. Once we finished, it was time to head to bed. Since Newark was an hour ahead, it became dark quickly so we decided to head to bed. DJ and I slept in Brianna's room while Da slept on the couch.

EFFECTS OF SOCIAL MEDIA

Yazmine McAboy

Social media connects our society because most teenagers find new friends through social media platforms like Instagram, Snapchat, and TikTok. Teenagers around UCS have made friends from different schools around Sumter County and even around the country by posting something about sports or showing their sports highlights. People connect through Snapchat with the cool filters. In a high schooler's opinion, a lot of teenagers use TikTok to make videos to have memories with their friends. Snapchat is a good option for people with long-distance friendships. It is a popular social media app because sending snaps back and forth updates friends on how the day is going. Some friends use Instagram as a way to create reels for their friends. These apps help people feel connected and not make them feel like they are alone. Social media gives people space to communicate and feel less isolated when they have no one they can talk to. Social media is not always a terrible thing.

Zamiyah Rice

Social media has branched its way off into society both markedly and materially. The majority of people's daily lives consist of social media, which has a detrimental effect on their mental health. It has been stated that social media influences the unfavorable behavior of some youth. TikTok, for example, has trends that target younger audiences. While most of these trends are perceived as vague, some are threatening and can lead to serious complications. Mental health is a big factor when it comes to social media. Situations like cyberbullying, explicit images being shared, and negative videos can cause one's daily life to be dull. If negative content is consumed regularly, it affects a person's mental health negatively.

Although there are bad factors of social media, there are some good factors as well. Since billions of people are online daily, small businesses are prone to grow more when they post their advertisements on social media. New ideas are shared on social media, which undeniably brings people closer. If a person knows the characteristics of social media, they can safely navigate through its complicated path.

Tamya Tolliver

Social media helps connect people all over the world. Apps like Facebook, Snapchat, Instagram, and other social media allow people to link to other people relating to their content. Facebook is a prime example of social media. When two people look at something on the app, FB connects them by recommending a friend suggestion on both accounts. It caters to people's interests and how other people relate to them.

However, it can also cause people to be lonely. One example would be Discord. Despite creating friendships, it can also destroy them. Friendships could be broken by one simple text or photo that leads to chaos, misunderstandings, and disputes. And just like that, anyone can become lonely again. All it takes is one mistake.

Amarion Dubose

Social media is basically apps where people around the world post photos and videos to show what they're doing. Everyone may think it's fun having social media, but at the same time, it can be horrible. The positive aspects of social media are that everyone can connect with their family and friends who live close to them or far away. It helps friends and family catch up with each other and creates a closer bond. Social media helps companies to let everyone know what their company is all about and broadcast what goes on there. The negative aspects are anyone can do anything to destroy or even call a person out to hurt. When an issue such as this occurs, it can be embarrassing, humiliating, or insulting because once someone posts it on their story, everyone will see it, especially if they are super popular on social media. The best choice is to have a private account, where no one can start trouble with anyone else.

Kamyia Dubose

Using social media causes people to be more lonely because of the time they are away from people. Sometimes, people get so caught up in their phones that they don't even realize it, something I can say is common from experience. Maybe it's because people are more entertained on their phones than actual people that they don't even mind it. Sometimes people can be really rude to interact with, so some people will avoid other people. Some will think that interacting on social media is connecting with people, but overall, you will not have any social skills in life, which will cause you to be lonely over time.

James Edmonds

Social media connects people together, and brings them closer. Some evidence to support this is people could be home and be bored and someone could send them a Snapchat and add excitement to their day. Another reason social media connects people is someone could live in a place far away from their friend, and their friend could post something on Facebook, and the next time those two talk on the phone, it would give them something to talk about. The last reason is if someone is having a party and someone does not have social media and that person who is hosting the party posts that they are having one on social media, then that person without it would be left out and could not go and have fun. These are a few reasons why social media can connect people.

Matthew Kendrick

Social media doubtlessly causes teenagers to be more lonely. For one, social media enables developing minds to insult and devalue each other. Facing the facts, kids are vicious creatures. They do not know any better than to make jokes that can often be dehumanizing at another's expense. Social media also quantifies a young person's value as a number on a screen. Be it followers, likes, or comments, young social media addicts completely value their worth as a human being based on how active their following is, how many likes each post gets, and how many nice or malicious comments a post receives. Lastly, adolescents cannot distinguish between online friendships and real friends. As humans are social animals, we depend on interpersonal relationships to survive and thrive. Online relationships are only a simulation of interaction with others. When the physical presence of another person is removed from the relationship, all that is left is an empty shell of a friendship, causing both parties to only feel more alone.

Addyson Tillman

Social media has seriously made its way into society since it was released. People have been affected poorly by social media. TikTok is an example of one social media app that has hurt society. TikTok is the backbone of toxicity on social media. People gain insecurities from the harshness of what is called a beauty standard. Society has a painful idea of what people should do and like, of what is attractive. People take a look at a video and feel negatively. Humans want to feel "pretty." Some of the people in our society have an eating disorder because of this. It has also caused a decline in face-to-face communication, which is crucial for people. People won't talk. Problems like these are real. They occur.

POSITIVE EFFECTS OF PANDEMIC RESTRICTIONS

Kayla Harris

Covid-19 was a deadly respiratory disease that affected millions of lives. During the outbreak, lockdowns became mandatory, and hospitals were too full to accept all patients. As a result, there became a shortage of health professionals, which further led to a crash in healthcare and a decrease in medical equipment and treatment for those in need. Although the primary purpose of implementing the pandemic restrictions was to prevent the loss of more lives, it further helped improve the mental health of those with social anxiety, allowed families to spend more quality time learning about each other, and presented opportunities for individuals to embark on new journeys to start or advance in hobbies and careers.

Pandemic restrictions helped improve the mental health of those with social anxiety. People with social anxiety have a great fear of socializing and interacting with others, especially strangers or those they are not familiar with. This disorder in kids can be seen as them lashing out in anger when they are extremely anxious or closing off their feelings. The learning of a child can be affected by the effect of social anxiety. Children can skew away entirely from activities that enhance the anxious feeling it gives them. "This includes obvious anxiety triggers like giving presentations, but also things like gym class, eating in the cafeteria, and doing group work" (Ehmke). The self-esteem of one can be heavily altered simply due to the thoughts of people watching and judging them. Similar can be said for adults in the workplace as well. For example, saying the word 'no' to a coworker can easily be challenging because the fear of being judged and embarrassed often times overshadows how they might feel about something. Quarantine opened a gateway to remote work and learning, so being within the comfort of your own home was a gift to introverts and people with social anxiety. It allowed people to have a more comfortable environment to improve their learning abilities, and motivation to work overall.

Pandemic restrictions allowed families to spend more quality time learning about each other. Before the pandemic, and even currently, some relationships within families could be rocky. With most adults coming home from nine-to-five jobs, and children coming home from school, there may be little to no time to talk about the day as the socializing candle had burned out from tiredness. A lot of people just want to eat and sleep when coming home, which is fine. However, the familial relationships inside a household can deteriorate over time if there is a lack of communication within them. "Families with healthy relationships make an effort to talk to each other and make sure each family member is heard" ("5 Factors To Building A Healthy Relationship"). When quarantine came about, it provided the perfect opportunity for families to come together and converse amongst each other. These much-needed conversations improved the knowledge of the lives of the people surrounding them.

Pandemic restrictions presented opportunities for individuals to embark on new journeys to start or advance in hobbies and careers. We all know starting a new path in your life can be difficult depending on the circumstances. Some may already have commitments to jobs, and others might simply just not have the time to start something anew. When restrictions began to be put into place, people were forced out of their usual routines. Having to stay at home meant that people had much more time to themselves to think, or perhaps, try out new things they have always wanted to do in the past.

For example, I have a passion for digital drawing. Before the pandemic, I was not able to draw as much as I intended to. But that changed when I finally had time to myself in quarantine to fully improve my art skills. Having a chance to start fresh or live out your dream was something not many could begin to fathom. It was like a car that would not move. The pandemic, however, was the gas that car needed to start that journey. These unexpected and unintended positive effects of the pandemic restrictions remind us to prioritize physical, emotional, and social well-being. When the opportunity arises, it can be extremely beneficial to use your time to focus on yourself and those around you. The pandemic was that much-needed thing to help people realize this.

III

Ourselves

POEMS

Anonymous

Teen Diabetic Poem

In a world of constantly counting, A young soul faces a life-challenging, Teen diabetic, a unique label, With strength and courage that is unbreakable.

From needles, pens, and glucose tests, A daily routine she must digest, Monitoring levels, highs, and lows, The battle against sugar's woes.

Amidst the teenage whirlwind, She gracefully handles what lies within, Balancing dreams with insulin shots, An unwavering spirit, tied in knots.

Challenged by labels, and misunderstood, She rises above, fighting every falsehood, For her pancreas may not produce, But her determination is nothing to reduce.

Teen diabetic, she wears it with pride, Through highs and lows, she'll never hide, Urging others to understand and see, That this condition doesn't define her – she's free.

Her strength shines brighter than any star, A warrior who's come so far, Unyielding in her pursuit of dreams, The power of resilience gleams.

Teen diabetic, a battle every day, Yet her spirit never fades away, She conquers the hurdles, one by one, Proving that she's second to none.

So let us celebrate her, loud and clear, A warrior who always perseveres, Teen diabetic, hear our heartfelt cheer, You inspire us all, year after year.

Addisyn Barton

Who Am I?

When introducing myself
What do I say
If I say what I want to
will they love or hate me
If I tell them the truth
will they look at it as a scam
But who am I really
Do I know
Can it be shared
or never shown
Will they judge me
Will I have to be fake
When they say mean things
Is it something I have to take
So the real question is
who am I and who are you

Ana S. Montaño Alanis

Dreamer

She sits next to me
    but she's not there.
    She is the breeze
through the bazaars,
the sounds
in the night,
the clouds
providing shade.
The close proximity
of inches
renders to a million words
invoked,
a thousand worlds
conjured
for her own pleasure;

To satiate her need.

She smiles at the

hidden possibilities
that the world has promised her,
secrets revealed
through each
conversion of a ray,
through each
reflection of the river,
but there is
longing
in her gaze.
A deeper sadness,
a deep restlessness.
A quiet fragility,
dandelions in a field and
dandelions in her hair
and at her feet
for every one of those
wishes she wants.
For all the things she craves.

She glances in my
   direction, but it's never truly at
   me.

Its beyond.

Beyond what I can give her,
   beyond what the world with its
   finite time
   offers.

ANA S. MONTAÑO ALANIS

That girl has
   two empty voids for eyes,
   forever longing to be filled
   with all the water in the world,
   all the space in the air,
   every grain of sand at every beach,
   every soft, warm embrace,
   every star formed in the history
   of the universe.

She is as hungry
   as the starved
   and as greedy
   as the rich,
   thirsting for a feeling
   long desired.
   Long spent
   longing a feeling
   long gone.
   Yet gone she isn't,
   but gone she might as well
   be.

Her roots are long,
   buried underground.
   It feels too late,
   or so she says,
   and so she stays.
   In that patch of grass,
   in the swaying trees.
   Camouflaged by the quotidian,

hidden in the normalcy.

But her habits betray her.

Even after so many years,
   her weary arms still manage to dissolve
   into the sky.

Ana S. Montaño Alanis

100

I like one hundreds a lot.
    I mean, it's a good, even, composite number.
    A perfect square.
A bit basic, sure, but easy to do mathematical operations with.
But more than that, I like receiving them.
I mean, who doesn't?
It gives us a high sense of achievement,
a "you did good" kind of achievement.
I like knowing that I did good.
That I did the best I could do.
That I can't do better
so I don't have to be better
because in life,
you can always be better.
You could always get higher.
You could always work harder.
You could always earn more.
You could always be nicer.
You could always improve yourself in a million different ways.

And a million is too much,
so I focus on one hundreds.
Because if I get one hundred,
I don't have to do better.
I'm scared of what will happen when one hundreds
don't exist
anymore.

Rebecca Boydstun

What is love-

What is love if not a feeling
   One of pain and sorrow
   A feeling of happy and sad

For the heart breaks and breaks
   Until this feeling of love is found
   Then and only then can the heart be healed

The heart shall smile, basking in this feeling
   And then and only then
   Shall the pain fade into a bitter-sweet joy

What is love if not a feeling
   One of bitter-sweet joy and fading pain
   For what you desire yet cannot have

Rebecca Boydstun

Love Breaks-

Don't fall in love, for what falls shall soon break
    And what breaks is my heart
    And my heart for you I give
Not to fall in love but to feel loved

The joy it brings to my heart
    To see the smile on your face
    And the light that shines through all that you do
    Not to fall in love but to see your love

Rebecca Boydstun

To be with you-

Was it destiny or fate?
    Was it just an accident?

    No meeting you was once in a lifetime
Bound to be together forbidden to ever meet.

All I do is dream and wish for your touch
    Knowing they will never come true

One day though they will come true
    My love for you is stronger than any distance

One day I will have you as mine
    In my arms but this time forever

No not destiny or fate
    Not an accident

It was love
   For it knows no boundaries

They say absence makes the heart grow fonder
   And that I now know is true

For the longer we are apart
   The more I grow to love you

No, it wasnt destiny or fate
   Nor was it an accident

Rebecca Boydstun

The dark-

The dark, not an enemy but a friend
    a friend there for comfort, there to listen

    The dark, all to me what is not to others
Not to hide but to show

The dark, home to the monsters
    Not the ones of fairytales, but those of this world

The dark, comfort and peace
    Holding onto me as I hold onto hope for the light

The dark, enveloping all that's around
    Canceling out the light and keeping me hidden away

The dark, my friend
    The one that I run to in my sadness

WISDOM WRITERS:

The dark, my enemy
   One that holds me from what I dream of

The dark, my comfort, and sorrow
   Where I dream and where I cry

Rebecca Boydstun

Girl in the Mirror-

ho is she? That girl in the mirror
   She can't be me
   For I have too many flaws no one loves me

So who is she?
   The one with long brown hair and green eyes
   The one in the mirror that everyone adores

No, she's not me
   She can't be
   For she is far too pretty

Who is she?
   Why can't I be her that girl in the mirror
   Why does she love me

She always smiles
   Always laughing
   And her eyes are like fields of green

I wish she was me
   Her long brown hair
   So soft and sweet

That girl in the mirror that I'll never be
   She shines in a brighter light than I
   And she's adored by so many

I wish the girl in the mirror was me
   I tear her down with every thought
   I break her spirit and dim her light

I see all her flaws
   I point them all out
   And yet she still smiles

She is still here
   Why is the girl in the mirror still here
   Why does she continue to smile at me
   For I have only ever been mean
   Does she still see me
   I am her and she is me

That girl in the mirror
   Her green eyes and long brown hair
   That's me I see

Why do I tear her down and rip her apart
   Why don't I love that girl in the mirror
   She once was so innocent

Her smile was so pure
   And I took that all away
   Now those green eyes full of pain

All because of me
   And how I can't come to love that girl
   All of her pain, I caused

Her innocence ripped away
   I am the cause of it all
   Me… Me… ME…

So who is she
   That girl in the mirror
   She can't be me

FEARS & ANXIETIES

Angel Burell

My biggest fear is failure in life. This is my biggest fear because I want to succeed well in life. My biggest goal is to complete high school so I can proceed to attend college. I want to thrive through my whole journey with a bang to finish well. I also tell myself, "You're going to fail sometimes in life and when you do it hurts, but then you have to put the negative thoughts to the side and think positive. Rethink the situation and go back to see what you did wrong and then try again and you will succeed."

My second biggest fear is being cheated on in a relationship. In life, most women do all they can for their partner in a relationship and the man still isn't satisfied with them. I honestly think if you aren't satisfied with the person, why stay with them in a relationship? You go be single and be happy with someone else. I honestly think sometimes men just stay with the woman just because she is beneficial. Men are going to always stay with the person who cares for them, but treat them bad by doing dirty things behind their backs.

Most men nowadays cheat because they think it is fun and it's a joke because they don't have a mature mindset. In my opinion, I think that you reap what you sow. Just because a man might cheat on you with someone else and you leave them, he goes with the person that he was cheating on you with and he thinks he is safe because he been had her. No, the man wouldn't be safe because that same woman will cheat on him and think of it. Then the man finds out he's going to wish he would've stayed with the woman who cared for him. No matter what you do in a relationship, god is watching you. You're going to get what you put down, but it will be worse. You might not get it back then, but it will come and hurt your soul.

Anonymous

Onism

Nothing nags me more than the realization that I'll forever be in this one body, one era, and one lifetime. I often look at people and wonder about their jobs, the goals that they have, the people that they love, and the problems they face. I look at old pictures of people and wonder what life may have looked like for them. What made them laugh? What brought them joy? Were they content with everything they had? Did they feel the things I felt? Then I think about how in the future, someone might look at a picture of me and wonder those same things.

It's scary that anything you do cannot be undone, any words you speak can not be sucked back into your mouth in reverse. Every day that passes, passes. There's no going back to yesterday and there's no skipping to tomorrow. All of the days will turn into months and they'll turn into years. Clocks just keep turning and turning until eventually, you're gone. Time doesn't wait for anyone.

I don't want any regrets in my life, but that's inevitable. Regardless of what you do, you'll make mistakes. Being aware of your mistakes and the people around you is just what makes you human. I find that poetic. Even so, it pains me as well. I know that one day my candle will go out. A hundred years on Earth isn't enough.

All of the people around me have lives. Like me, they have stories and plots that'll someday come to an end. Is it possible to experience everything and all things at once? I know how people affect me, but how do I affect other people? You can understand a person but you'll never see it from their respective perspective. You'll only just see it from your own. You can be no one else but yourself.

I feel trapped, stuck, like I'm in some sort of prison. I want to know what things look like for the other person. How they might feel or how they perceive everyone and themselves. I want to know what it's like being a different species, race, or gender. Why do people have the mentalities that they have? What's under the layers of the person I see them as? No amount of words can describe one person or anyone.

We change constantly, nonstop. Every second, we soak in the things around us like a sponge. We adapt to our environment. It's the way we're wired. It makes me wonder, what if I wasn't born in America? What if I was born in Africa or someplace like Japan? What if I was born a guy or a bird? What if I were a different race? What if I were born in the past or the near future? Would I still be me? What makes me, me? It's a foreign feeling, something that I've never been able to describe. Onism? Yeah, I think that's the word.

Onism - the frustration of being stuck in one body, that inhibits only one place at a time

Kayla Harris

I can't exactly just choose one fear. I feel like they are all on the same level but I know for sure being by myself and dying are definitely at the top of the mountain for me. I am going to start with the being by myself one because it is kind of hard to explain. For starters, here is some background. I can say I am a bit of a loner. Any chance I can get to get away from a crowd, I will take. Any opportunity to be in a room by myself at home, I jump on it. It may sound weird or mean to you, but whenever I'm at home with my family, I stay in the living room. I call it "my area" in the house. It is the only room I can be in by myself in. YES! Not even my bedroom is somewhere I can call my own because it is my younger sister's room as well. Let's get back to the living room though. Whenever I can be in there, I feel like I can be more open with myself, show more emotion, do what I want without anyone there to judge me. However, this is where it may sound mean.... I hate it when someone comes through the room. Whether it be to go to the bathroom or kitchen on the other sides, it just irritates me to the max! I just don't get it. I think it may be due to the fact that whatever quiet, dark body of water my mind is sinking in, gets violently pulled out of it the moment someone invades my space. I know it may be stupid to claim a living room to myself but that's just me.

Now let me go back to the fear aspect of this. I came to conclusion that I like to be alone but not by myself. It's a feeling I've struggled with since childhood, feeling like I was never fully accepted or understood by those around me. Being by myself is a constant source of tension and anxiety for me, and I often feel uneasy and uncomfortable in my own skin. Just knowing that I am completely by myself in a location, with no other person there kills me. It's a feeling that I've learned to manage over time, but it still remains a significant source of fear and discomfort for me, and it's something that I'm constantly working to address and overcome.

Ok! Now the second fear, dying…. I know, I know, it's such a cliche answer but whenever I think about death It literally stresses me out with the amount of things that are just completely unknown to a living person. It's a thought that I often try to push away, but it always seems to resurface in times of uncertainty or when faced with life's challenges. Dying is a concept that can be difficult to comprehend or wrap my head around, and it often brings up feelings of unease and anxiety. The idea that my life can just end at any moment, with no warning and without the ability to control it, is deeply unsettling, and it's something I struggle with regularly.

I will say though, that a new series on YouTube really changed my perspectives on the afterlife and I honestly believe the things I saw while watching these videos. The channel is called *Sam and Colby* and the series is called 'Hell Week.' I know what it sounds like but stick with me. It was something they did for a 10 million subscribers milestone and because it's close to Halloween. Basically, they would stay in the conjuring house for a week, and when I tell you the things they saw and experienced are things you simply can not debunk. I can't explain everything but I really recommend it because it gave me a little closer look at what the afterlife is.

Zy'Kirea Long

Let's be real, our biggest fear is death. I'm not really scared of it because it's a part of life. But going 6 feet under in this dark hole is just so terrifying to me. I am fearing the pain of loneliness or just not existence, even the unknown of death. Just the thought of being alone at a grave catches me off guard. It is something I just started to believe in now because both of my aunties are gone, and family members are gone. In the bible, God says even though I walk through a valley of death, I fear no evil for you are with me, your rod and your staff, they comfort me.

Aliyah Martin

One of my greatest fears is speaking publicly in front of a large audience. I am surprisingly comfortable in a setting where I am required to communicate with 20-30 people. But speaking in a room of 100+ people often makes me anxious. Ever since I was in middle school, I have had trouble participating in inter-school competitions, and I think that fear stuck with me. It does not affect my day-to-day work but does make me apprehensive about leading conferences and seminars. To remedy this, I have signed up for public speaking courses that teach techniques to overcome these fears and build confidence. I feel that they have helped me a lot, and as I continue to practice with them, I am hopeful I will overcome this fear for good soon.

Another one of my greatest fears in life is rejection. Not being chosen for projects, not being included in team activities, etc., makes me feel rejected, and while I understand that it is not personal, it is just a fear that occupies my mind. I have always been an introvert and had a tough time making friends in school, and those experiences have led to this fear in me. But I am trying to overcome this feeling and feel better about this fear by journaling, rationalizing incidents that make me feel this way, and voicing my fears.

Ana S. Montaño Alanis

My biggest fear is the dark. I know, I know. Very generic. Very common. Almost all kids at one point in their lives have this fear. They say—adults I mean—that it goes away when you get older. When your mind can say, "Well, this is probably me tricking myself into thinking that there are things in this dark," and rationally evaluate that you are, in fact, in your room alone. And that's true. They were right. It did get better as I grew up. However, I can't really say that I overcame that fear.

It lingers in the shadowy corners and comes out late at night when my mind can't say for sure that those sounds it heard didn't originate from an identifiable source. It comes out when I am walking down a corridor, safely surrounded by walls, but for some reason, I can feel a presence near me. It's right behind me, in the spots where my eyes can't see. And when I turn around, it moves, quicker than lighting, out of the spot I'm facing and behind me once more. It breathes down my back and watches me as I debate whether to keep my pace and pretend to be calm or walk faster until I break into a run to get to my room. It watches me from the window, whenever I forget to close the blinds, peeking through the curtains and watching my figure slowly cover itself with more of the blanket. It's waiting for me when I'm taking out the trash late at night, and it's that precise moment when I finish placing it and turn around to face the house that it runs after me. It chases me, its footsteps thumping on the ground as loud as the pounding of my heart as I run back to the house. But I was expecting it. I always knew it would chase me the moment I turned around, so I always won the race. Turn, run, open, close, and *click*, lock the door. Even when I close my eyes as I lay down, I can feel it staring at me, its face hovering above mine. I don't dare open them.

But sometimes I do. I turn around and confirm, yes, in fact, there was nothing there. My mind knows that there is nothing there. At least, that's what I tell myself. I don't think I'll fully convince me.

Hannah Prince

My biggest fear is tryphobia. It makes my skin crawl every time I look at it. If you don't know what it is, it is tiny holes on people's hands, food, and plants. Why is this my biggest fear? Every time I look at it it makes me itch, and the scary part about it is that some people can scratch their sleeves to the point they might bleed or leave a scar that's how bad it is. So that's why I try not to look at it. This might be my biggest fear.

My second biggest fear is getting played while in a relationship. It is very scary because you give your energy and affection to someone who you thought loved you. This is how it starts. They tell you they love and a couple of weeks or months later they tell you that they do not want you or you find out that you're getting cheated on. That is the worst because you really loved the person and they treated you like you were nothing. And they don't care anything about your feelings at all, just leave you there hurting. It would be better to come face to face and talk about the things that we did or what things didn't work out, but some boys or men are childish and don't want to do anything. They just want to go from one girl to another, which is very immature. That's showing you they are not good for you, and they just love to play with girls' or women's hearts like it's cool. That's why some girls like me have trust issues. Every time you think you can give your trust to someone, they do something that will break that trust. That's why it's hard for me to trust any dude these days. That is why you need to trust the Lord and pray, and I promise you he will find someone that's right for you. Wait and be patient.

Traeger Stephens

I feel uncomfortable in elevators because I fear getting stuck by myself. My sister once was stuck in an elevator on a trip. She had to call the fire department to come get her out. She was stuck for a long time. Once, I was at the beach on vacation with my dad and some other family. I went to our place to get a Dr. Pepper and was on the elevator alone. When the elevator doors opened on our floor, I ran out between the people waiting to get on. I always take the stairs instead of using the elevator.

Avery Long

Everyone has a fear, whether they know it or not. Fears can be as simple as not making an "A" on a test, thunder, or even shots. That might seem small to you, but it can mean a lot to others. A few bigger fears might be failure, rejection, or even death. My biggest fear in life is not being accepted.

Ever since I was little, I have been the "black sheep" of my friends. I was always that one person who wasn't wearing the "stylish" new clothes or name-brand clothes. I wouldn't be invited to a lot of things, although I always invited everyone. I felt like a loner. I was scared I wouldn't be accepted for who I am when I got older. I don't want to be alone and by myself when I grow old. I want to have friends who I can enjoy and spend time with.

Now that I am a little older, I feel safer knowing I have my friend group. My fear is still not being accepted. What if I go to work when I get older and they don't accept short people? What if when I go to college, someone doesn't want a diabetic as a friend? My fear will always be not being accepted. I'm short, I'm a diabetic, and I have always been the one to not put myself "out there". What will happen in the future? I guess we won't know until we find out.

Tavares Foster

I have a few fears, most small like my fear of the dark. It's only a minor fear and it just makes me a bit uncomfortable. I used not to be afraid of the dark when I was younger and still living with my grandma. I even used to stay up at night playing my Xbox, not even caring how dark it was. One night, however, I looked back and saw barely anything, it was just pure darkness and it creeped me out.

Another fear of mine is bugs touching my skin. Although I'm not scared of bugs, the thought of them crawling on my skin makes me feel uneasy. I actually like bugs a lot, especially spiders and beetles. Although I have never held an insect before, thinking about feeling their puffs of hair and exoskeletons creeps me out. Overall, I find insects fascinating, but I don't want to touch them.

Lastly, this fear is kind of irrational and weird but not unreasonable. I have a fear of someone being behind something, like a door or curtain, and attacking me. I think it started when I was little and I was watching a horror movie. It got to a scene where a guy was walking around his house looking for an intruder and eventually ended up in his bathroom. The door to the bathroom was opened in a way that the guy couldn't see the intruder pass the door and the reflection in the mirror. The guy walks in, doesn't see anything, lets his guard down, and gets murdered.

Leia Pitre

My biggest fear is heights. I don't know why I have this fear, just that I struggle with going anywhere high. Stairs to second-story houses are scary until I get used to them, and rope bridges should be a crime. If we were meant to go high, we'd have wings.

Addyson Tillman

I have anxiety regarding a lot of things, be it a fear of being left alone, or a fear of something as simple as spiders. I have amaxophobia, which is the fear of driving, but none of these are as severe as one of my other phobias. I am terrified – no, mortified of thinking of my own death. This is the phobia known as "death anxiety," or by its title, thanatophobia. I honestly do not know how to pronounce that. I cannot remember when I obtained this fear, but whenever I think of death, I start to panic a lot. It is like a mini panic attack. I hate the idea of death so much. My fears are so, so small compared to that one, and I, honestly, am scared of life itself.

What do I worry about? I worry about a lot of things. Some can range from the less important things to the more harsher things. Sometimes, I wish that I could just stop worrying about everything because it makes my stomach churn and spin with a really bad dreadful feeling that I absolutely cannot stand. Anyhow, one of my worries was a simple course change, the other being death itself.

The course change worry – I do not even understand why my nerves did all of that to me. It felt like it was performing somersaults and twirls in my tummy every time I thought of having to switch my classes. This change was not a choice. I had to do it. I would be at home just worrying about it for no reason… Okay, going into a class without your close friends sounds a bit disappointing, but I went overboard. When I walked into my new class, I realized I had actually been worrying about it for no reason at all.

My biggest worry is the one that I have accepted the most – death. When I think about death, it is an unpleasant feeling that arises inside of me. I hate the way it makes me feel because I am just full of dread. The repulsiveness of that emotion is so high for me because it is just uncomfortable and upsetting. I know I'll pass one day, but I tend to cope with my feelings by joking around. Usually, I will just say that I'm immortal or I will live to be one hundred and thirty years old. It helps a bit. My anxiety for this just feels like I am worrying for nothing, even when something tells me I worry for everything.

A.J.

Social anxiety and anxiety in general is a big part of my life. As I got older, I learned how to deal with it better, but when I was younger, my social anxiety used to be at high rise. When I was younger, I was terrified of going into stores by myself. If my mom tried to send me into stores, I would try to avoid going in there or go as fast as possible just so I don't get seen or stopped. Now that I have two jobs, a cookie business and a job as help at a local City Hall, I will sooner or later get over that fear. In my job at the City Hall, I have to communicate with people who come in and need assistance with their water bills and more, so I have to talk to them. I have been working there since the summer, so I am getting better at communicating with people without feeling scared or anxious. I still feel like that from time to time, but I do agree that working is helping me get over my fear. At the beginning of my second job, running a small business was tough for me. I would say the part that was tough for me was when I first started and I had to market my cookies. I was forced to put my cookies out there and communicate with people to get more recognition. When it came to talking to people, I was scared about what people would have to say about my business, that I would get judged and wouldn't get supported. I prayed over and over and still pray about my business to this day and the fact that I kept God in my business. It is doing excellent as of right now and I'm forever grateful. When I hosted my first event at the Mardi Gras parade here in Livingston, I was a vendor there. I had no idea how I was going to do it. I was nervous so I prayed the night before. I knew that I was going to meet so many new people that I would have to communicate with, but it was a great thing my mom was right by my side through all of this and she helped me ace that event. I had no idea that we were going to sell out of cookies that day, but we did and I'm forever grateful. I was so nervous when we first got there because in my head, I was like, "'We're not gonna sell out," saying that because I genuinely thought we weren't, especially because that was my first big event. Not knowing that I was completely wrong we did and gained a lot of new customers. Pushing past the anxiety, in my opinion, helps me grow my business and stay positive. Having social anxiety is stressful but at the end of the day going through it and still experiencing it helps me grow into a better and stronger person.

Zamiyah Rice

As much as I would like to adore my art, I can't. Maybe it's because I compare myself to others. Maybe it's the evil work of the internet, but whenever I try to improve my art, I get frustrated. It's hard learning new things, I lack a lot of patience. I get that it takes practice, but following through with it is a pain. Things are different than when I was younger, learning how to draw an eye for the first time. I reminisce on all the fun it was to create something. Now as an older teen, I feel my talent rotting away into nothing.

Caroline Sparkman

Am I too hard on myself? I have been told that I am by lots of people, and the sad thing is that I know it's true. The truth is that I try to act like I am strong, but I am scared of what people think of me. I have lots of anxiety, and it just hurts sometimes. I feel like all eyes are on me, but I didn't care what people thought of me when I was little. Now, I feel like I'm the center of attention, and even now, writing this, I have a feeling of anxiety about what people are going to think about reading this. I hope that this helps people in the future, and maybe even know. Still, words can't explain how I feel. People are just not nice. When you get older, you start to be able to read people and their intentions. It's sad and devastating. I just feel like people should be good to one another. I know I have my moments, but I try no matter what because this generation is something else and not in a good way. I just hope this all changes when I go to college.

Zy'Kirea Long

I always used to worry about not having the life I planned for myself. Not getting the dream job I want. Not being able to help the people around me or even buy my dream home and live alone, having asthma. What if I have an asthma attack and can't get my medication? What if I can't pay a bill? What if I can't buy a car? What if I'm not smart enough for my future? I always think about my life and what it will be like when I'm older. But the Bible says in *Matthew 6:34 Therefore do not be anxious about tomorrow, for tomorrow will be anxious for itself. Sufficient for the day is its own trouble.* Now I trust in God with my future because worrying about it now could keep me in the past.

Amarion Dubose

Self-esteem: Do I have It or Need to Gain It?

The biggest problem I have is, of course, my self-esteem issues. I'm the type of guy who wants to make everyone smile and please people with my special skills. I often question whether I'm the good type for a certain group of people to be friends with or if I am too timid or shy to be around them. My best decision was just to be my nice and kind self to everyone because I realized that how I treat people makes them like me, though I'm different.

Sometimes, when I'm at home, I just stare out the window, wondering about My Hometown, a new job, and working on my social skills because I'm a senior in High School and about to graduate in a few months. When I think about these situations, I want to ask my parents how I can make all of these happen, and they will just give me advice on how I should have a game plan to succeed in life.

I would sometimes suffer from people talking and spreading lies about me, especially when hearing about it from someone and not knowing that it happens. When I found out about the incident, I cried myself to sleep, knowing that I was in a situation that I was probably never going to escape from. Now it's all over, but I do sometimes think about it, and I would still get upset about how everyone betrayed me. My parents told me that I should just ignore it because I'm a senior in High School, and the only thing I should do is finish the rest of this out, graduate, and focus on my future.

There are days I'll go for a walk and think about the future. When I think about it, I wonder how to make things happen, such as taking action to achieve a goal or bring out a desired outcome. I want to accomplish many goals before I graduate high school, but sometimes I run into problems trying to complete them. The majority of the time, I'll be so excited to achieve them and would get a bit impatient. I realize it takes time, and the only thing to do is wait and take one step at a time.

Ana S. Montaño Alanis

Sometimes meaningfulness comes and stares at my face when I'm lying down on my bed waiting for sleep. Maybe it's because, when there is no particular focus, your mind starts to wander. Mine first wanders to my day, since it's almost over. I think of what I have done. Actually, instead of thinking on what I *have* done, I think of what I *haven't*. Maybe my brain is just wired to think that way. I could try to find a positive light for it since my brain is always thinking of what else I could do, but it really isn't. It weighs down on me because I know especially well that I don't like to do things. Or maybe I do, actually. Maybe I do like to do things, but I like doing some things better than others, and when the teachers in the Wednesday Kickoff tell us to remember to make each day meaningful I get a cold splash of water on my face and wake up as I fall asleep and realize I might not have done anything meaningful today.

For something to be meaningful, it has to have meaning. It has to be something that matters, but what if what I do doesn't really matter? I mean, I finished a book today. I completed my assignments on time throughout the week. I even won a soccer match yesterday. But does it matter? Does mattering enough to be meaningful also have to matter to others? Because maybe some people will care a little, and maybe some others will care more, but many, many, many more people will not care at all. Maybe more than 99% of the world will not care at all, and won't find some kind of interpretation or application for it in their lives. Can something be meaningful if it doesn't matter to the world?

Can something be meaningful if it matters to me? I hope so. It would be much easier. Yet, at night, I can't shake the feeling that it doesn't really matter what I did because I could have finished a lot more. Unless I did something like writing a book, or creating a cure for a disease, or inventing the microwave, then it really doesn't matter. All of the things I did during the day were reduced to nothing. Nothing of value or of worth that I could offer to the world, and so sometimes I think that the world sees me as someone with nothing of value to offer.

It's a very depressing and negative way of thinking but I think depressing and negative things on depressive and negative days. And sometimes, those days are finished with depressive and negative thoughts. However, I *am* a well-rounded, controversial person, like most humans, and I do know that I *am* exaggerating to a point. It definitely feels like I'm exaggerating, especially when I describe things on ink and paper, figuratively speaking. So, I quietly think to myself before I drown in the infinite possibilities of *could* and focus on *have*.

I *have* finished reading a book today.

   I *have* finished my homework.

   I *have* taken a test today, which, if I might add, I think I did pretty well on.

   I *have* talked to my friends and made jokes, and it was pretty fun being at school with them even though it usually feels like we do nothing and accomplish nothing during it, which is really ironic because if I focus very hard, my time in school is rarely like that.

I think like that because I try to only think of what matters. Why would that matter? But it does, doesn't it? It matters to me at least. Maybe it's not enough to be meaningful, but at least it means something to me. It means the difference between how I end my day, and maybe even how I start my morning and how I continue my week. But actually, maybe underneath all that, I'm still sad and negative. That's okay too, I guess.

I suppose it's okay because I do know that even if I don't do something that matters every day I know that *I* matter. At least, that's what my parents always tell me :)

INSECURITIES & BODY IMAGE

Hannah Prince

The part I try to hide from others is my anger issues. This is because I don't want people to see that side of me, so when people make me mad, I try to distance myself from them because there may be people around, and I don't want them to see me like that. Also when I'm angry, my emotions take over I'm not the same anymore I don't want to hurt people. I want people to see my nice, goofy side. But I got better with my attitude because last school year it was bad, so the summer, I made a goal to work on my attitude and how I treat people. What helped me achieve my goal is my best friend, two of my other friends, and also their mom.

Kayla Harris

To be honest, I've always struggled with feeling at ease in my own skin. I can't help but notice how short I am and wish I could grow a few inches taller. What about weight? I've never felt as though I weighed as much as I wanted to. Society's beauty standards frequently make me feel as if I fall short, literally. When I'm dealing with insecurities about my own body, it's difficult to see taller and seemingly more 'ideal' figures portrayed in media and culture.

There's this constant pressure to get rid of things like hip-dips, those lines that seem to set me apart from the perfectly smooth bodies on social media. The stretch marks resemble maps of my growth and change, but I sometimes wish they weren't there. Don't even get me started on my teeth; I've always wanted them straightened because I feel self-conscious when I smile. Recently I just got them scanned for Invisalign, something I had been yearning for years now, and get my trays soon. Although I can't help but feel guilty for some reason. They were really expensive and it kind of hurt to see my mom pay so much for something I don't necessarily need. Not to mention, my little sister somehow managed to get her braces done that same day so she spent well over the amount she originally planned for JUST ME. The media portrays these flawless individuals as if they are airbrushed, making it difficult not to compare myself and wish for those changes.

Media and culture have a big influence on how I perceive my

body. The constant depiction of 'perfect' bodies as the norm creates unrealistic expectations. It's a constant struggle to accept myself as I am while also feeling pressure to conform to these unattainable standards. I even began working out a few months ago to try and achieve MY ideal body. I usually keep to myself about my insecurities because I feel like I am not taken seriously or something along those lines. For example, when my little sister is insecure about something, my mom will baby her to the max. I can never even imagine getting that type of treatment. Despite the difficulties, I am attempting to embrace my individuality and acknowledge that beauty comes in all shapes, sizes, and imperfections. But some days it's more difficult to block out those idealized images that make me doubt my own worth.

Hannah Prince

I'm comfortable with my body. There are always some people on social media that will Photoshop their body or sometimes use filters. I feel like us ladies shouldn't Photoshop our bodies just to make them look like they're dream bodies. It's OK to have stretch marks and it's OK to have belly fat. That's beauty. Also, some ladies do it for men and I feel like you should not change your body for men. A man should love *you*. If you have to change your body or anything for a man, then they are not right for you. And I feel like it can affect our ladies because they are going to hate their bodies. After all, they see other ladies with the best-looking bodies. But it's OK to be you.

Angel Burrell

I am very comfortable with my body. The only thing I feel uncomfortable about my body is my having eczema. By me having eczema, I can't wear certain shirts because there's a spot on my left shoulder. I used to be really embarrassed about it when I was younger. Now, I look at is a beauty mark, and it resembles me. Many times I have felt bad because I thought I was overweight. I was bullied during my younger ages because there were big girls in my class, and they always tried to make other girls like me feel bad because they weren't pleased with themselves and because they were overweight. Once I got older and realized that they did that because of jealousy, I wondered why they would be jealous of me. There are many people in life who may hate your guts just because they want to be you. In my opinion, I don't understand why people hate so much. Just because you aren't passionate about yourself doesn't mean you should bring others joy down.

PASSIONS

Avery Long

I am very passionate about Photography. Photography is important to me because I love to capture those special moments for others. Being able to capture those moments and know that I happened to be the one to take them just makes me so happy. My love for photography started when I was little and I would watch my aunt take pictures for families and more. She inspired me so much to the point I would model for her just to watch how the camera works and how to pose others.

I started wanting to do photography recently. Last year, I took two classes that involved photography: Digital Media and Yearbook. The first semester was the best experience with taking pictures, which eventually led to me getting a camera for Christmas. Since Christmas, I have done sports, birthdays, senior, family, and more photoshoots. I am slowly building a business like my aunt did. Photography is my safe place and it holds a special place in my heart.

Ana S. Montaño Alanis

I am passionate about passion.

I guess that is the only way to say it. Like "loving love" and "being afraid of being afraid", I am passionate about passion.

Why wouldn't I be? I love being passionate. It's impressive. Imagine wanting something so much that you go out there and try to reach it. Try to claim it. Try to walk one step forward at a time so that the goal gets closer and closer to you.

Passion makes you try, and that's very impressive because sometimes it's hard to try. Or at least, try with enthusiasm. Many people can try to, well, try, but it takes a special kind of someone to try, and try their best. Every time. For everything. For the things that are important to them. And they keep on trying even though others tell them to stop, and the time spent wanting tells them to stop, and sometimes when even themselves tell them to stop.

Because at that point, it's not just a want. It's turned into a passion.

Passion, defined by Oxford languages, is a strong and barely controllable emotion, as well as, an intense desire or enthusiasm for something.

An intense emotion. An intense desire.

A want stops becoming a want simply because the word *want* is too small to contain the desire. At that point, it has grown into something so big that it can't be compared to what it once was. Stopping a want is a million times easier than stopping a passion because, at that point, a passion is part of you.

You are what made that passion yours. You put a piece of yourself into what you were doing, and you admire yourself for it. It is important to you because you are important to yourself. And because it is important, you keep on working on it. You keep pursuing it because it has become an immaterial extension of yourself in other things. You cannot think of it without thinking of yourself. You cannot think of yourself without it. And all of those lines of separation that scientists say are from the empty space that partakes in atoms try to tell you that you will never actually touch it. But there's a secret.

You have.

You *have* touched it. In your dreams, you can see yourself standing there, and it is important to see yourself standing there because that's when you actually feel it. You feel complete. You are no longer fragments. You have achieved reuniting with the little parts of you you have left on the street as you walked by and on the air as you breathed. In every careful action you have taken to achieve your goal. Your passion. It was a part of you because you were a part of it and now you're together again. And you love that sensation, because we, as humans, want to make ourselves whole.

Then you wake up, left with the phantom feeling of being everything. So you get up. Out of bed and into your clothes. And you walk outside, ready to chase your pieces down.

And those that are truly passionate know that their pieces also want to go to them. They've seen it in the way opportunities arise if one is willing to take them. If you put in enough time, enough effort, those fragments of you start being rekindled in familiarity. They know you are part of them. They are part of you.

And everything wants to be whole again.

I wish I could say I had passion. Maybe I do. Personally, I think it's just a heightened version of want. Of longing.

But I think that's a good start.

I am willing to make it a good start.

I want to be able to do what I wish to do but I find myself forgetting about it. Forgetting to dedicate time and space and care and productivity. And sometimes I wonder if it could even form into a passion. I mean, *is* this really important to me? *Am* I really that motivated?

Am I fooling myself?

Into trying to be something, anything, so that I can say that I did amount to something. I could do it, even if it's not what I like. Even if it's anything. Anything other people can look at and say, "Wow, you really achieved something there, buddy," and "That's impressive."

I did *achieve something. It is impressive, thank you. I* do *amount to be a whole person, I tell you. I swear I do. Don't I?*

Do I? Is this really my passion? Could this turn into my passion?

Then I remember why I started doing it. And I guess I laugh off those tiny doubts and they bounce back on the bed, fall down the covers, and crawl beneath them. Because I'm pretty sure wanting something that makes you happy is a great start to a passion. So I get up. Out of bed, and into my uniform. And I walk outside, ready to chase it down.

Because it does sound quite nice to be in the places my dreams take me.

FAMILY & HOME LIFE

Anonymous

Being your big sister is so confusing. I'm always stressed, no one listens to me, and no one respects me. But when Mom and Dad are gone, I'm in charge. You can all cook, clean, bathe, and get dressed by yourselves. But you want me to do it, or make sure you've got everything before you do anything. You fight me, you treat me like I'm stupid, you disrespect me on the regular. But if I say you're wrong, if I prove you wrong, if I disrespect you back, I get the bad end of a belt. You hate me except when you hate someone else more. But I love you, and want what's best for you and I know you love me too even if I can't feel it. You yell. You wake me up fighting or screaming for a reason no one really knows. But I make sure my bedroom door and your bedroom door are open just a crack in case you need me in the middle of the night and I make rounds when most of you are asleep to see if you're okay. You make me mad, you insult me, you make me feel worthless sometimes. But I'll do it right back at you because you think it's funny and I like making you laugh. You'll tell me you love me and hug me, then ask for a favor. But you can't get up from bed to put your dishes in the sink even if I said please. You'll throw things and hit me, and push me and mess up my things. But mom won't let me punish you, because when I was 8, I took it too far and hurt you. No one lets me forget that, ever. I feel awful for what I put you through as kids and I'm glad you didn't get spanked or slapped as much as I was because I was a bad child. But I wish you were punished for your bad behavior and I wish you learned from seeing what happened to me. But you were too little and our mom learned that it wasn't okay to leave welts on our legs and bruises on our bums. I'm glad that when mom's voice shifts, you don't worry about what you did wrong and I'm glad when dad comes home angry, you all accept that he needs time to relax. But I am scared of disappointing them, I'm always saying sorry, even if I didn't do anything, and to prove myself I based a large part of my personality on being good in school and being smart. You guys can get C's and all that's said is "Do better." But when I was your age, a C got my fun books taken away and I had to stay inside studying to make the grade up with extra work. I could still go over to anyone's house before that, but that option was also taken away. You didn't get the worst of the bullying when we were younger, you didn't have cuts or bruises or attempts against your life. But the bullying you did experience is my fault, because I was weird, and grieving, and I didn't know how to handle my own bullies' words, so when it transitioned to actions, I became a little monster. I didn't know how to handle depression and anxiety, so I did the oddest and craziest things I could because I thought it would make people leave me and you alone. It didn't. I still threw myself in front of those older boys though, I shielded you from the punches and scratches, I made sure they couldn't reach you and I didn't move even when those hands were around my throat stealing my breath and I made sure I took every hit. I made sure your ugly drawing was okay so Mom and Dad could tell you it was beautiful and hang it on the fridge. I don't know if I'm a good sister, I don't know if I'm even a good person most days, but I do love you. You know that right? You know I care about you, you know I helped raise you because I love you right? Some days I don't like you at all, but I love you. I can't do much else for you in this world other than help you learn and try to protect you, but you know I'm trying right? It's really confusing being your big sister, but I wouldn't give up any one of you for anything.

Anonymous

Mom, is it love when you blame everything wrong in the house on me first because I was never a really good child to you? Is it love when you tell me the awful things you went through growing up and talk about how you never had a childhood when I try telling you that I'm struggling with my mental health? Is it love that makes you so angry when I can't be as successful as you expect me to be? Is it out of love that you live through me because you never allowed yourself to be who you wanted? Is it love when you talk about not being here and then beg me to stay with you? Momma, is this the love you know? Is this the love you meant to give me?

I have so many questions, Mom what makes you think I hate you? What made it okay for you to tell me things that a daughter shouldn't know? Why do you often hurt my feelings and tell people you don't know why I'm so sad all the time? Why do you tell me secrets that are so heavy I can never hold my own because of them? Mom, why do you yell all the time? Why do you act like the world is out to get you? Why are you so proud of me in public and so piercingly critical at home?

My whole childhood, I was raised by three versions of you, three moms in one body. The Authoritarian, who believed in corporal punishment, who yelled at me to the point of making me cry and wet myself, who took what I loved because they were privileges and I was not what you wanted. The sensitive Supporter, who cried at a moment's notice, who would comfort me when I had bad dreams or hurt myself, the mom who cared about my feelings and spoiled me when no one else was around and we were alone. And finally, the Child. The parent who watched cartoons and bought plushies because you didn't have that, the mom who acted like a teen well into her thirties, who took all the blame but none of the responsibility, and who was fun on rare occasions when everything was okay.

Mom, I love you, but is it love what you do to my mind? I want to stay and help you get better. I want to be there when you're sick, and I want to have a healthy relationship with you. But Mom, at the same time, I want to get away from you. Sometimes, I only want to be where you cannot see or reach me. I know you raised your mom, but can you see the cycle repeating? Mom, you've grown into a different version of your mother. Is this cycle your love?

Avery Long

Decisions for me are very important but hard to make. I have made many decisions in life, but a recent one I had to make is whether or not to help out a friend in need. I am one to always be willing to help out a friend or family member in need. I want to be the one known to save everybody. Although I can't do that, I can try my best to help others out.

I met this friend about four to five years ago here at school. We became good friends through one of my best friends. Three years ago, this friend–we can call him Lake–became my new best friend and we started getting along really well. This friend has been there for me more times than I can count and has been the sweetest soul to me. Recently, Lake has been through some family issues and needed guidance and help. His parents are divorced and he lives with his mom. Recently, his mom hasn't been there for him and has basically abandoned him. She doesn't do his laundry, cook for him, or even come to his games. He feels sad. Lake is hurt. Very, very hurt. I have tried my best to help him be happy and get stuff off his mind, but it's hard when the parent you live with doesn't care about you and cares about your siblings more.

Lake brought the idea up of living with me at my house since we have become close and my mom adores him so much. He and my brother are best friends and sometimes I believe they're more friends than us. I had to decide if it was a good idea or not and, of course, run it by my mom and both his parents. I decided, since I wanted him to be happy and he deserved to stay here at UCS and not move away, that the best thing would be for him to move in if he wanted to. Even though I had to make a decision if it was a good idea or not, Lake then had a harder choice to make. In order for him to move in, he had to give custody to his dad. Luckily, his dad agreed to take custody and let him live with us to finish out high school. Lake has been a little sad lately because he had lived with his mom since he was born and moving away from her will be really hard. Lake is doing so much better, though, and I am really glad to make the decision to allow him to stay and live with me. I would do anything for my friends, and I am glad Lake trusts me enough for that decision.

Ana S. Montaño Alanis

I have an amazing family and two amazing parents. I honestly believe that I must have hit the jackpot when I was picking a family to be born into because they're *that* great and cool. They support me on a lot of things, are always disposed to enroll me in extracurricular activities, and push me to achieve more. Their pushes (in my *professional* opinion) are quite healthy and metaphoric. They aren't the type of parents to *actually* push me down some stairs or off a cliff. All in all, yes, great, beautiful parents.

This, however, does not mean that they let me slack off. If they did, they wouldn't be good parents anymore because parents have to raise their children to be able to face the real world. They *have* to have some "respectable" expectations for me. Right? I think so and I believe that they think so too. I think that I think that way because that's what they told me. Were they told that too?

Either way, I have expectations to meet, and they're…lenient, I guess? They probably would not be mad unless I was failing a subject. I don't know. I have not really gotten to that point. I don't really remember them telling me, "Hey, get good grades, and don't fail!" It just felt like a given, you know? The way others don't remind you that you shouldn't breathe in water. You just know, or, at least, you can guess. So I try not to breathe in the water and work well. So I do well. I get good grades.

Then I take it further than it needs to be. No, if you want to talk about pressure and expectations, let me tell you about the biggest inflicter of them all: myself.

I believe somewhere along the (time)lines of essays and arithmetic function, I started basing my self-worth on my grades. A good student was equivalent to a good person, and I knew that good persons were good daughters, and if I was a good daughter, my parents would love me. A bad student disappointed others, and therefore, wasn't loved.

Which, by the way, newsflash, isn't true. One can be loved or hated regardless of how well they do academically, professionally, or financially.

Nonetheless, it felt that way, and I didn't want to take chances. I prioritized my studies above all else. To be frank, it was... surprisingly rewarding. I loved getting 90s and 100s and coming back with a penned happy face in the upper right-hand corner of my papers. It felt good to be rewarded for all my effort with a delighted smile, and there was no higher honor than earning a place in the ever-full surface of my dear refrigerator.

However, when middle school started and getting good grades seemed more important than ever, the new 1, 2, 3, 4 system rocked my world washing machine style, completely inundating the fabric of my life. At first, it was excruciatingly hard to get a 4 on anything that wasn't math. Nothing was rounded up. Nothing. If I got a 3.9, I was expecting that 3.5 on PowerSchool. I did, however, get lots of threes. But threes are equal to eighties, which aren't nineties and most definitely aren't one-hundreds. Being the person that I forced myself to be, I wasn't about to leave it at that.

Determination and persistence are great qualities to have as long as they don't turn into stubbornness.

Throughout the course of that year, I had a lot of negative thoughts about myself. I didn't believe myself capable of many things, and many times referred to myself as stupid. I wonder why I did that. Putting myself down, of course, would only push me further into the whirring water surrounding me and would only succeed in speeding up my slow asphyxiation. I think that maybe I wanted to punish myself for failing to get that question right, for failing that test, for failing my expectations. If internally screaming at myself hurt me, then that was a fine retribution I had to endure for my wrongdoings.

Is it wrong to not know something? Is it wrong to fail? Reflecting upon it with more maturity, of course it isn't. Most will say it isn't, and yet no one said it to me. Who can blame them? I didn't know the question, much less the answer.

That year, I passed all of my classes with at least a 90 in each, with the exception of History, where I got an 89.6 which got rounded down to an 80. Yes, it still irks me, but even I laugh at my petty irritation. I've heard many people mention the truism, "Pressure makes diamonds," but don't let that make you forget that it also crushes people. Learn to administer healthy pressure in the form of goals and deadlines. That is, *realistic* goals and deadlines. Understand that failing is preferable to not trying, and if you ever need help, there are people, who are most definitely not paid enough by the government, who would love to explain things and dedicate time to you. Teachers are just wonderful like that.

LOSS

Aliyah Martin

It was just my sister and I for a while. I was a really bright and extroverted child. Even though there were only the two of us and I had always been an only child before her, I loved my sister. The year 2021 brought the loss of both my mother and the loss of a part of myself, and while I had always been a happy and attractive child, my moods began to change. I wasn't really interested in anything beyond 2021 because I didn't know what I wanted to accomplish with my life. For a young child like me, it was a very scary period, and I was also very sad since I had just lost my mother. Recently, everything has gone well. But even though I've adjusted to my new life, I still often think about my mother and the realization that I've forgotten how she sounds. This makes me sad. My sister is 2 years old, and she was around 6 months old when our mother passed away. I often wonder what it would be like for her to grow up without a "mom"... Just thinking about how we all have to look at our memories of her and also teach Amori about her mother through memories makes me feel so awful. Right now, my dad is raising all three of us daughters by himself, and he is doing an amazing job. While I try to be strong for my family, it hurts to know that my mother is in that grave. We often visit her there. Recently, I've been happy with my life because everything is going well, yet since I was a child, a lot has changed.

Caroline Sparkman

Recently, in November, I lost my dog. I always knew that they came and went, but I truly believe that they are like family because, unlike friends and people, you think you know dogs are always there for you. They pick you up when you are down and are always there for you when you cry. When she disappeared, I was so sad that I felt like breaking down. but I have learned recently that you do not truly understand what you have till it's gone and it truly hurts. It's a terrible feeling, and I hope no one will ever have to feel that. I also had a terrible dream that made matters even worse. It was about us finding her and then her being abused and it hurt me when I woke up because I didn't know where she was, and it hurts to think what could have happened to her. I still do not know where she is; no one deserves to go through this.

Acknowledgments

Hello! It's impressive that you have gotten all the way to the back, especially more so if it has been after you traversed through all of the different styles of writing, perspectives, opinions, and feelings of adolescents currently attending University Charter School. I applaud you. The only reason I got through that was because I, for one, was the editor, and two, felt dedicated enough and crazy enough to volunteer to edit the Wisdom Writers.

Without further ado, I would like to begin these acknowledgments by recognizing Mrs. Morgan Allen, who is infinitely patient and gracious enough to let us organize this book through her time. Even through all the complications of having what most would consider a "free class," she still found the opportunity to let those who wanted to write, write. I would also like to give her a special thanks on my part, since she extended that grace to me time and time again, even though the final draft for this project kept being pushed further and further behind.

I would like to acknowledge Paris Henderson, who began this idea. She is graduating this year, so if you see her or recognize her, tell her it's a mighty impressive feat she has accomplished in our school; a true personification of the word, and our mascot, "trailblazer."

I would like to acknowledge all of the students who have taken the time to put their thoughts into writing, and for being brave enough to let us include them here. Regardless of your decision to include your name under your work or leave it anonymous, you have all shown

ACKNOWLEDGMENTS

more than enough courage. In their commemoration, and as a more interesting way to list names that may or may not hold any meaning toward you, each student who has taken part in the Wisdom Writers this year will be listed with a six-word memoir written by them.

We acknowledge the students:

Amarion Dubose
 Mississippi born, School student, Senior Class of 2024 Today.

Jaylon Amerson
 Born in Tuscaloosa, grew up in Wendyhills.

Jayar Mitchell
 Born to bleed green, future lawyer.

Preston Irby
 Mississippi born, Alabama moved, composer today.

Zamiyah Rice
 Alabama-born, has sisters, art and writing.

Ella Hill
 Fairhope born, Art, Music, lessons learned.

Lennon Phillips
 Demopolis raised, and I enjoy friends.

Carmine Paris
 I've liked being with my friends.

Teyanna Rush

WISDOM WRITERS:

Guam-born, Alabama-raised, future nurse.

Miriam Griffin
  Sip born but Bellamy raised now.

Aliyah Martin
  Alabama, very active, University Charter School.

Andavien Bell
  Demop born, Livingston raised– Sports today.

Evan McCrory
  Demopolis born, Livingston living–music lover.

Jarron Jackson
  Mississippi born, Bama raised–future NFL.

Amari Jackson
  Georgia born, 2 jobs, life's good.

Jamaya Jenkins
  Demopolis born, York raised– basketball today.

Rein Tidmore
  Born to live, born to love.

Milleigh Grace Kloysuntia
  Mississippi to Alabama, always busy and eating.

Zykeria Long
  Born to paint, raised to help.

ACKNOWLEDGMENTS

Tamya Tolliver
  Livingston resident, former athlete, UCS senior.

Anonymous
  Mississippi born, Alabama raised- Human today.

James Edmonds
  Alabama born, duck hunting, football, fourteen.

Anonymous
  Moved a lot. Staying until graduation.

Madison Love
  Senior, planning for after high school.

Anonymous
  Cali born, Bama raised, athlete today.

Craig Ellington
  Love life, regret nothing, cherish everything.

Caroline Upchurch
  Born to party, forced to work.

Ana S. Montaño Alanis
  Unstable background, unknown future, moving forward.
  (An alien, but you'll never know)

Lastly, we thank you, reader. Know that from the simple act of buying this book, you are helping our school, and if you have taken the time to read it, we hope that you learned something, or at the very least that you felt something. Our mission was to create a book that could impact the lives of others, so we hope it has, even in the slightest, etched a mark onto you.

www.ingramcontent.com/pod-product-compliance
Lightning Source LLC
LaVergne TN
LVHW051036070526
838201LV00010B/222